The Complete
ST BERNARD

PAT MUGGLETON,
MICHAEL AND ANN WENSLEY

RINGPRESS

RINGPRESS

Published by Ringpress Books Ltd,
PO Box 8, Lydney, Gloucestershire GL15 6YD

Discounts available for bulk orders
Contact the Special Sales Manager at
the above address. Telephone 01594 563800

First Published 1992
Reprinted 1998
© 1992 MUGGLETON AND WENSLEY

ISBN 0 948955 864

Printed and bound in Singapore
by Kyodo Printing Co

CONTENTS

Pat Muggleton with Ch. Bernmont Victoria and Ch. Bernmont Warlord at Blackpool in 1969 when her dogs won the dog and bitch CCs.

Michael Wensley with (left to right) Ch. Swindridge Ferdinand, Ch. Swindridge Madam Danielle and Ch. Swindridge Sir Dorian.

INTRODUCTION

St Bernards have been part of Pat's life for almost as long as she can remember. Her earliest canine companion was Whiskers, whose pedigree was somewhat doubtful, resembling a cross between a Bearded Collie and an Old English Sheepdog. Whiskers came into the Muggleton household in wartime when Pat's mother, Enid, enticed the hungry stray home with morsels of food. He remained a devoted friend until his death in 1950. Rob Muggleton was the main instigator in the purchase of a St Bernard, as he had always wanted to have a large dog, so a visit was arranged to the Daphnedene Kennels of Horace and Daphne Ayckbourne in Norfolk. Enid and Pat would gladly have changed their minds as they walked up the drive flanked by the kennels, housing enormous dogs. However, they were enchanted by the puppies and a three-month-old bitch was purchased for the princely sum of 25 guineas. Thus Daphnedene Ramona became the foundation bitch of the Bernmont Kennels, jointly owned by Pat and Enid, until Enid's death in 1983. Rona still holds the record for the longest lived of either the Bernmont or Swindridge Saints, reaching the grand old age of fourteen years! She started her show career by winning a first prize, with Pat winning best child handler at the same time. It was at this show that Mrs Walker of the Peldartor Kennels suggested that Rona should have a litter, and she suggested their stud dog Ch. St Dominic of Brenchley as a possible mate. Three puppies were retained from the resulting litter, and in 1953 Cornagarth Recorder, a son of the Swiss import Ch. Cornagarth Marshall van Zwing Uri, was purchased. Brumas resembled his father, being very continental in type, and although greatly admired by foreigners, he found little favour in the English show ring. From this beginning the Bernmont Saints increased and flourished, housing many Champions. In 1969 Ch. Bernmont Warlord won the Working Group at Bath Championship Show – the highest honour a St Bernard had won for eighteen years in the United Kingdom. Several imports have joined the Bernmonts over the years, and the kennel still carries more continental than English blood. Pat has also kept Dalmatians, Cockers, Poodles, Parson Jack Russells, and still has Cavalier King Charles Spaniels. Pat won Best of Breed twice at Crufts and judged the breed there in 1981.

Mike and Ann started the Swindridge St Bernards in 1971. Mike had previously had a Bull Terrier in early childhood, but it was not until he bought Ann a Border Collie as a birthday present that he

Ann Wensley with Swindridge Ebenezer.

became involved with dogs. Ann had been brought up with a dog in the National Children's Home. She started work as a kennel maid for a vet in his canine hospital and boarding kennels, and moved on to work in racing greyhound kennels. Wendy, the Border Collie, was joined four years later by Bruce, a Labrador who used to go shooting with Michael. Both dogs were good companions for their daughter Julie. When Wendy died, aged ten, Bruce was joined by their first St Bernard, Andlyns Duchess Delicia (Rosalind). She was not a show dog, and was not used for breeding, but she did well at Obedience and enjoyed it. A few months later they acquired another St Bernard through their veterinary surgeon. This was Snowranger Your Delightful, who became the foundation bitch of their kennel – and eleven Swindridge Champions are descended from her. In 1986 Mike, Ann, the Swindridge Saints and several cats joined Pat and Rob. The combined kennel is highly successful, and the Bernmont and Swindridge Saints have now been joined by a flock of Pedigree Rouge de l'Ouest sheep and a fold of Highland Cattle – they are bred under the combined prefix of Bernridge.

Chapter One

HISTORY OF
THE ST BERNARD

The St Bernard has perhaps the most romantic history of all dog breeds. Everyone thinks of it as the rescue dog of the Great Saint Bernard Pass in the Swiss Alps, although, sadly, they are no longer used for rescue work. Modern technology in the shape of the helicopter has made them redundant. The Swiss rescue teams, who fly in to help injured skiers on the mountains, are usually assisted by the much lighter German Shepherd Dog. Travellers no longer need the Hospice of the Great St Bernard as a vital shelter in the mountains, and it has become a tourist attraction, keeping a few St Bernard dogs for the visitors. The Great St Bernard Pass was once the main route between Italy and Switzerland – through Aosta on the Italian side to Martigny on the Swiss side – a distance of twenty-six miles. Today, a motorway passes through a tunnel in the mountains; the tunnel is four miles long, cut through solid rock, and in the middle of the tunnel is the customs post on the Swiss/Italian border. The mountain pass is only open for three months of the year – usually from June 21st to the end of September – but this is very dependent on the severity of the weather. Even when the road is clear, there is danger from avalanches from the snow above. The Hospice stands over 8,000 feet – 2472 metres – above sea level. The surrounding mountains are even higher, and snow can fall as deep as thirty-six feet. The lake on the mountains is frozen for 265 days out of the year, and even in a hot summer the temperature never reaches much above 60 degrees Fahrenheit, and it can

The Hospice of the Great St Bernard is now a tourist attraction.

                                    Hospice of the Great St Bernard.

fall to minus 22 degrees. It was this inhospitable terrain that Hannibal encountered when he first crossed the Alps with elephants in 218B.C. One hundred and fifty years later, Caesar went to war and the Romans conquered the valley up to the Rhine. Within fifty years Augustus had made a road through the Alps to join Aosta and Martigny. On the top of this pass they built a temple to their god, Jupiter, and a refuge for their soldiers. When the Romans went to war, they were accompanied by their war-dogs, known as Mollossers. These dogs, which were also used to protect livestock, had come from Greece, taken by Alexander the Great from their original home in Asia Minor. The Romans adopted them, and took them everywhere they went. One hundred years after Christ these dogs were used to guard all the mountain passes and Army posts in Switzerland, Austria and south-eastern Europe. There were two types of Molosser: one was light in built and light in colour, with a long head and free movement, and was used as a sheepdog. The other type was heavier in build, dark in colour, with a strong head and short muzzle. The Illyrian Molosser had prick ears, and the Babylonian Molosser had pendant ears. Both the Mastiff, which was used to guard monasteries in Tibet, and the St Bernard can be traced back to the Molosser. In fact, the St Bernard used to be known as the Alpine Mastiff; other names attributed to the breed include Bari hund (bear dog), Hospice dogs, and

The early St Bernards that were trained in rescue work at the Hospice.
Hospice of the Great St Bernard.

Bernhardiners, as they are still called in Switzerland today. When the Romans retreated from these regions, they left the descendants of their dogs behind. The valleys below the Pass of Mont Joux, as it was now known, became their home. The Roman temple to Jupiter was destroyed by Saracens in 950A.D., and the remains of the old military post became the hiding place of robbers and bandits.

The real story of the the St Bernard starts at the end of the tenth Century, following the birth of the man who was to found the Hospice of the Great St Bernard. Bernard of Menthon came from one of the noblest families in Savoy, and after finishing his education in Paris, he went to Aosta to became a priest, refusing to marry the bride his parents had chosen for him. Eventually he became the Archdeacon of the Saint Augustine Cathedral, which stood at the foot of the Pass of Mont Joux. The Pass was used by all manner of travellers: soldiers, merchants, men looking for work and pilgrims en route to Rome. Many never reached their destination because of the blizzards and intense cold, besides the brigands who plundered in the mountains. Bernard was horrified by the tales of some pilgrims, who had sought shelter in his Cathedral after being attacked on the pass. He decided that, with the help of the villagers, he would build a hospice as shelter for travellers on this treacherous route. There were small shelters halfway up at Bourg St Pierre on the Swiss side, and San

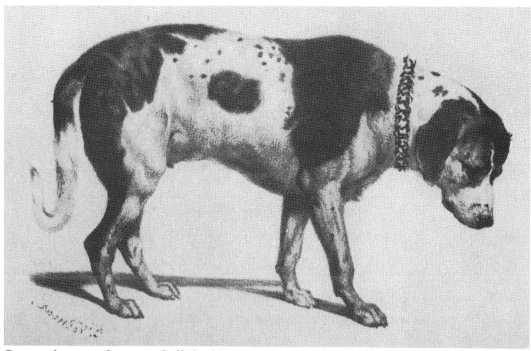

Barry, the most famous of all the Hospice dogs.

Barry, re-mounted in 1923 in a noble pose, is on display at the National History Museum at Berne.					*Hospice of the Great St Bernard.*

Remy on the Italian side, and the Cloister at the Hospice was eventually founded in 980A.D. It became a place of refuge for anyone who needed it – rich or poor – and there was no charge. The pass thus took the name of its founder, Saint Bernard, for he was later canonised. The Hospice was enlarged over the years, with the help of donations from Bernard's wealthy family and other nobility. The monastery was founded in 1049A.D. and Bernard died in 1081 at the age of eighty-five.

Unfortunately a fire destroyed all historical documentation in 1555, and there is no written record of the existence of dogs at the Hospice until 1707, when there was a note to say that a dog had been buried. However, there are two paintings attributed to Salvator Rosa, in 1695, which depict two dogs – obviously St Bernards – one mantle-coated, one splash-coated; both had excellent heads. Most historians believe that the dogs were brought to the Hospice around 1660, and were descendants of the Roman Molossers. They were brought from the valleys, and to begin with, they were used for protection, although it is hard to believe that they were not taken to the Hospice much earlier, if only as guard dogs, particularly in view of the bandits in early times. There was certainly no other form of protection for the monks. However, it was not long before the monks discovered that the dogs had an excellent sense of direction, and a very strong sense of smell. They could locate a man buried under six feet of snow, and could find their way on the treacherous snow-covered mountain passes even in dense fog. There is a coat of arms, dating from 1350,called De Hailigberg, which portrays a dog's head that is similar to a St Bernard. In translation, De Hailigberg means 'Holy Mountain', and some believe this was the insignia of the monks themselves.

The first written evidence which describes the work of the monks and their dogs comes in 1774. Travellers write of the monks going out daily, accompanied by their trained dogs, to look for people that were lost or injured, and they would then guide them back to the Hospice. The dogs could dig a person out by themselves, if they were not buried too deep under the snow. In 1787 there is a record of the dogs warding off an invading band of robbers and saving the monastery's treasures.

Barry, born in 1800, was the most famous of all the Hospice dogs. He is reputed to have saved over forty lives in twelve years. At the earliest hint of fog or snow, Barry would become restless. If he could not manage to dig out anyone buried in the snow by himself, he ran back to the Hospice to get help from the monks. One of his most famous exploits occurred in the March of 1806, when Anna Maria Vincenti was returning to Italy with her young child, following her husband's death. She was penniless, and she could wait no longer to make the hazardous trip home to Italy. There was no snow in the valleys, and she knew she could find shelter on the way at Bourg St Pierre, and she would get food at the Hospice. Brother Luigi, who had

Many artists have portrayed the St Bernard at work. This picture, 'The First Aid Team of the Great St Bernard', was painted by E. Leubenberger in 1893.
Hospice of the Great St Bernard.

trained Barry from puppyhood, was out with him in the morning when Barry stopped, as though listening. Suddenly there was a roar like thunder, Brother Luigi threw himself to the ground next to Barry, and the avalanche rolled past them, leaving them unharmed. Brother Luigi decided that they must go back to the Hospice and let the Prior know that they were safe, but Barry refused to return. He had never been disobedient before, but eventually Brother Luigi was forced to return

The Hospice St Bernards at work.   *Hospice of the Great St Bernard.*

alone. Barry did not come back that day, and the monks feared that he was lost. Before retiring for the night, they had a last look outside the massive walls, and there was Barry, huddled by the wall with a bundle on his back. They took him into the warm hospice kitchen and undid the bundle – it was Anna Maria's child, wrapped in her shawl. She had tied it to Barry's collar in a desperate attempt to save her son. The monks managed to revive the frozen boy, and he survived, even though his mother had perished in the avalanche. Barry was to suffer a terrible blow when

Brother Luigi failed to return from a mission. The dog was sent to find his master, and he eventually discovered Brother Luigi lying in a gorge, after he had slipped and fallen. Barry could not pull his master out, so he ran back to the Hospice for help. Sadly, by the time the monks came to his aid, Brother Luigi was dead – no one knew whether he had been alive when Barry first found him. After his master's death, Barry spent much of his time working alone in the mountains. In 1812, when he was twelve years old, he went to help a man in the snow who mistook him for a wolf and stabbed him. Barry persisted in trying to help him, and was stabbed repeatedly. The monks found them and carried them both back to the Hospice. After careful nursing, Barry recovered, but he was never fit to work again and was sent to friends in Berne to spend his remaining two years in retirement. By then he was famous, and when he died his body was presented to the Natural History Museum at Berne. The first attempt to mount him was poor, and his head hung down in a dejected manner. However, in 1923 he was restuffed and mounted in the proud stance that he still holds today.

The great Napoleon Bonaparte had reason to be grateful to the St Bernards. When he crossed the Alps in 1800 ten of his men fell down a crevasse, and no one was able to reach them. The dogs and the monks came to the rescue. They hauled the men up and took them back to the Hospice. It is said that Napoleon patted the dogs, and to show his appreciation he financed similar hospices on the Simplon Pass and on Mont Cenis. The keg or brandy flask round the St Bernard's neck was made famous by Sir Edwin Landseer's painting The Rescue, but in fact, these were not used in rescue work after 1883, for the monks carried all the first-aid equipment. However, there are early references to small wine-holders being attached round the dogs' necks by travellers in the early 1820s. The Hospice has records of two Newfoundlands being brought from Stuttgart for training as rescue dogs, and in 1830, St Bernards were crossed with the Newfoundlands, and this produced the long-haired variety. It was at first thought that the long hair might help them in the freezing conditions, but in fact, the ice stuck to their coats, and balls of snow formed in the long hair on their feet, making them unsuitable for work, so all the long-haired dogs were given away to friends in the valleys.

The Pass of the Great St Bernard was used by kings, noblemen and peasants, and all were given help and refuge. Over two thousand people owe their lives to the dogs at the St Bernard Hospice, and it became famous worldwide. The Hospice dogs became known as St Bernards in the nineteenth Century, and they received a number of royal visitors. Queen Victoria stayed at the Hospice for a night, and so did her daughter, Empress Frederick of Germany, when she visited the region in 1882 with her husband, who was then the Crown Prince. Later her son, Edward, visited the

The arrival of the helicopter signalled the end of the St Bernard's role as a rescue dog in Switzerland. *Hospice of the Great St Bernard.*

Hospice when he was eighteen. The Hospice is now a tourist attraction, and is a must for all devotees of the St Bernard. We went there towards the end of September, and within a few days the drop in temperature was so noticeable we needed winter coats. The dogs were housed within a stone building, and they were in long narrow wooden kennels, with a single dog in each kennel. They all had raised wooden boards to lie on, and they looked comfortable and contented. However, there was a campaign in the German Press to improve their conditions, and they have now been put in larger kennels behind glass – whether the dogs are happier is debatable. The visitors themselves are well catered for with an hotel, restaurants and gift shops. Most are on the Swiss side, but there are one or two cabins with souvenirs on the Italian side. There are also many souvenir shops on the road up to the Hospice. However, a statue dedicated to Saint Bernard de Menthon stands on the mountainside, and so amidst all the trappings of the tourist trade, we are still reminded of the remarkable work of this great man, and the many lives that were saved by the St Bernard dogs that are named after him.

The St Bernard is a wonderful companion, but make sure you weigh up the pros and cons before taking on this giant-sized breed.

Chapter Two

CHOOSING A
ST BERNARD

The St Bernard is the most majestic of all breeds, but you should be aware of the advantages and disadvantages before deciding to share your life with one. They are lovable companions and ideal pets, but they are large dogs and a lot depends on how tolerant you are as to the amount of space that is required. They do sleep quite a lot, but when standing, a Saint is the height of a table. It is advisable never to feed a St Bernard at the table, as they do drool a lot, and if they rest their head on the table-cloth they will slobber all over the edge of it! The tail-end can be equally disastrous; a wagging tail can sweep ornaments off low tables and shelves. Of course, the well-trained St Bernard should know his place and stay where it is told at mealtimes, or be put into another room. If you have an open-plan house, it is advisable to have suitable outside accommodation for times when you may have dinner guests or visitors who are not doggy-minded. It is also handy to have somewhere for the dog to dry off, if it has been raining, and somewhere to wipe its feet before allowing the dog back into your best room. It is useful to have a towel always nearby to mop up the drool – if a Saint shakes its head it can go up the walls or even on the ceiling!

· Food is another important consideration, and you must be confident that you can afford to keep such a large breed – a big male may eat between 4-5lbs of meat a day. Surprisingly, they do not need a lot of exercise. Most will be content with playing in the garden and going out for short walks, which should be regarded as a training exercise. All Saints are different, and some will enjoy a walk more than others. The British-bred tend to be heavy and they do not want to go very far, whereas the American and continental type are more energetic. So if you want a dog that will walk for miles, it is unlikely that a St Bernard will suit you. Another important consideration is to decide what you will do with your dog if you are away from home for long periods of time. Obviously, this is not an ideal situation, and before you take on a St Bernard – which is a dog that needs companionship – you should seriously consider whether this is the right breed for you. If you are away a lot, and you are still intent on owning a Saint, we suggest that you get a second dog to keep the other company, as one dog left on its own all day would be very lonely and miserable.

When you have finally decided that you are going to purchase a St Bernard, the first step is to contact a breed club, and find out the dates of forthcoming shows. If you go to a big show, preferably a club Championship Show, you will be able to see all the leading exhibitors and decide which type of St Bernard you prefer. Watch the judging, and talk to the exhibitors, but make sure you are not too strongly influenced by what people have to say. If one breeder is openly criticising another, it is not worth paying attention. People of integrity would not behave in this way.

MALE OR FEMALE?

When you have decided which type of St Bernard you want and you have found a suitable breeder, you will then have to wait until the next litter is available. In the meantime, you can decide whether you want a male or female St Bernard. A male is usually bigger, heavier, and much stronger than the female. Both sexes of the breed are equally lovable, and it is largely a matter of personal preference which one you choose. However, there are certain pros and cons which are worth weighing up. A male will not leave patches on your lawn when he is older, which can occur when a female urinates. However, a male does seem to spend all day lifting its leg, urinating on everything in the garden. The female tends to urinate in one flood – and she generally has her chosen spot for this. As a result, the lawn can become yellow or discoloured. Whichever sex you choose, try to teach the dog where you want them to do their toilet.

Males seldom moult more than once a year, whereas a bitch usually moults twice – she generally comes into new coat with her season. A bitch comes into season every six months – a few come in more frequently, others may go longer between seasons – but if a bitch has a season as often as every three months, it can be a sign of disease of the reproductive organs. A bitch that comes into season too frequently is usually sterile. The red or blood discharge of the season lasts for about fourteen days, but she remains attractive to males for up to seven more days. The majority of bitches keep themselves very clean, and the season will not cause you any trouble, but if you have a large enough garden, keep her within the confines of your home. If you have to take her out, be careful to go where there are no other dogs, and, if possible, drive out of your area, as you could have male callers outside your gate. All in-season bitches smell alike to all dogs – large or small – and there could be a small, but hopeful suitor on your doorstep.

Males are no problem throughout the year, unless they are very bitch-minded and get the scent of a bitch in season. If you have only one dog as a pet, unless he is an exceptional specimen, it is advisable not to use him for stud – what he has never had, he may never miss. If you want to keep two St Bernards, you should either choose two of the same sex or, if you want opposite sexes, you must have the facilities to separate them when the bitch comes in season. The alternative to this is to have the dog either spayed or neutered. The English Kennel Club has recently ruled that spayed bitches and neutered males can be shown, despite the stipulations of the Breed Standard, but this ruling only applies in the U.K. Two adults of the same sex can fight, but this is unusual if they have been brought up together. Opposite sexes will nearly always agree with each other.

If you are hoping to breed with your St Bernard there is not much point in buying a male, unless you already have your own bitches. People do not take their bitches to an unknown stud dog. Your male would need to become a top winner before he would be in demand at stud. A bitch is a far better prospect if you want to start your own kennel. Of course, you can never be a hundred per cent sure that she will breed, but there are very few bitches that are completely sterile.

TEMPERAMENT

As well as the physical differences in type, there are variations in temperament which should be considered when choosing your St Bernard. The St Bernard generally has an excellent temperament and loves children, but most dogs will be protective towards their owners, particularly the continental dogs – after all, their first task was as guardians of the Hospice. The English type tend to be more docile than the continental type, but the heavier-built quiet dog often does not live as long as the more active continentally bred dog. The continental type, which is prevalent in America, is highly intelligent, and it can usually walk the English type off their feet.

An eight-week-old puppy showing excellent hind angulation.

PET OR SHOW DOG?

It is important to tell the breeder exactly what you want your dog for. Do not say you want a pet, if you are really looking for a potential show dog or a brood bitch, in the hope that you will get a bargain. Some kennels sell puppies to pet homes much cheaper, and this may often be because they are without the official breed papers. This would usually be the case if the puppy had an obvious fault, such as being mis-marked. In Britain, white around one or both eyes, or a half or a full-white face would be considered as serious faults. In Europe and America a dog without a white blaze, or one with a black face would be unacceptable in the show ring. In fact, black faces rarely occur outside Britain, as this type has been largely excluded from breeding programmes elsewhere. A blue eye is taboo in all countries. This is also known as a wall eye; it is a condition in which the surround of the pupil is blue, rather than brown. A blue eye is a definite fault in the St Bernard, although it is acceptable in the Collie and the Old English Sheepdog. It is a congenital fault in the Saint, although it does not affect a dog's sight or its overall health. An experienced breeder might use a mis-mark to preserve a line which would otherwise be lost, but no one would ever use a blue-eyed dog or bitch for breeding. A breeder may also be prepared to sell an older puppy, that has not turned out to be completely sound, for a nominal fee as a pet – again without official papers.

RESCUE DOGS

Pet dogs may also be obtained from rescue organisations, but you must be either very lucky or very experienced when it comes to getting a dog from this source. There are some lovely Saints that come up for rehousing, but there are many that go to the rescue centre because they are unmanageable – all too often because their original owners didn't bother to train them. It is wise to avoid a dog with an obscure background, unless you are prepared to tackle any problems that may arise. Good kennels will usually take back any of their own stock that has become homeless, and they will make a thorough assessment before rehousing the dog with suitable owners.

SELECTING A SHOW PUPPY

A puppy can only have show potential, no one can give an absolute guarantee as to how it will look when it grows up. A male puppy must be entire: it must have two testicles descended in the scrotum. A monorchid is a male with only one testicle, and although he is capable of reproducing, the condition is hereditary, so it is unwise to use him at stud. A cryptorchid is a male with no testicles; he is incapable of reproduction, and is suitable for a pet, only. The testicles can usually be felt by eight weeks. If there is no evidence of them by the time the puppy is three months old, it is most unlikely that they will descend at a later date.

A puppy with show potential should have a strong square-looking muzzle; it should never look snipy like a Collie. It should have a good stop, and it should look strong, thick-set and sturdy. An eight-to-twelve week old puppy should not look rangy, although older St Bernard puppies do go through some awkward stages while they are growing – at five months some St Bernards can look most ungainly. It is important to bear in mind that the biggest puppy will not always make the biggest and best dog. In fact, the very large, heavy puppies are most prone to leg problems. Some of the smaller puppies are just slower to mature, and they can finish up better than an enormous pup. The front legs should be well-boned and straight. A problem sometimes found in the heavier puppies is that they can go down on their pasterns, i.e. walk on the back of the ankle (the front leg between the knee and the foot). This condition can usually be corrected with exercise and extra calcium, but if you are a novice owner, always seek veterinary advice. Excessive supplementation of either calcium or vitamins can be as bad as insufficient quantities, and can lead to serious bone damage. The use of steroids should also be avoided.

When you are assessing a puppy, check that the legs on each side are parallel to each other. The hocks on the back legs should not turn in towards each other – this is termed cow-hocked – and the stifles should not appear to 'sink' in. Sometimes both these conditions are connected with hip dysplasia. Unfortunately, this is a bone fault which affects a very large number of St Bernards, to some degree. Dogs cannot be hip-scored until they are over twelve months of age, and so this is an area where you have to rely on your own judgement, or enlist the help of someone that is experienced in the breed. Other causes of bad movement are patella problems, i.e. the knee on the back leg, and also loose hocks. A Saint can also tear the cruciate ligament in one or both hindlegs, but this does not appear to happen to puppies, but rather to the young adult. The problem can be corrected by surgery and controlled exercise. However, you should never buy a puppy that appears to have leg troubles, unless you only want a pet, and you know what you are taking on. A Saint that moves badly can still make an excellent pet, but you should not have to pay a top price for one whose legs are unsound when you buy it.

The perfectly marked puppy has a white blaze between the eyes, a white muzzle, and a white collar or part-collar round the neck. In fact, the white collar is not considered a very important point in Britain – there have been many Champions with hardly any white collars at all – but it is an important marking in America and on the continent. A show puppy should have a white chest, white legs and feet, and most of the tail should be white – from the tip upwards, with only the root being brown in colour. The body can be full mantle – all-over brown – or splash-coated – white with brown patches; both body colourings are permitted in the Breed Standard, but some judges prefer a mantle coat. A few judges like a lot of white on the body, particularly in America, and it does look very flashy when it is clean. The other head colourings are brown, with black or darker shadings, particularly on the ears. The nose or nostrils should always be black.

LONG-HAIRED OR SHORT-HAIRED?

In Britain you will see a wide variation of type in the breed, and you must decide which type you like. The smooth or short-haired variety is not as popular as the long-haired (rough) in Britain and America, even though this type was the original St Bernard. However, this may change, as, increasingly, owners seem to prefer a low-maintenance, easily-groomed dog, and the short-haired requires little attention, other than regular grooming, to keep it in top-class condition.

Johan van het Wapen van Capelle of Bernmont, imported from Holland.
The rough or long-haired variety is more popular in Britain and America.

Ch. Denbow Miss Muffat, owned by Dennis Owen.
The smooth or short-haired variety is easy to care for.

24

Chapter Three

TRAINING A
ST BERNARD

Training a St Bernard puppy should start as soon as possible, for remember – that lovable ball of fluff could one day be as heavy, or possibly even heavier than you, and if it is not well trained and well-behaved, you will not be able to control it. All dogs should be taught to behave well and in a sociable manner so that they can be taken out and can mix with people without being a nuisance. A badly behaved dog, particularly one as big as the St Bernard, is nothing but a pest, and will never be the enjoyable companion you are hoping for. Start to teach basic obedience as soon as you get your puppy. If you do not want it to follow you through a door, tell it to stay; if it pushes by you, fetch it back. Never let the puppy think it can have its own way.

The first essential is house training, i.e. toilet training your puppy. Fortunately, most puppies learn this very quickly, especially if you are consistent in your training. Put the puppy out into the garden after every feed, every time it wakes up, before you go to bed at night, and at any time when the puppy appears restless. Stay with the pup until it 'performs', otherwise it will not understand what is required, and then give it plenty of praise. If you catch the puppy just as it is about to make a mistake in the house, correct it with a sharp 'no' – a word it should know the meaning of from the start – and swiftly take it outside. It will soon get the right idea. However, young puppies cannot always last through the night, so leave some newspapers by the door, and hopefully, the puppy will confine itself to using these.

Pat Muggleton with Ilona v Spruitenbeek aged three months. Training should start as early as possible with a big breed.

A St Bernard puppy must learn to walk on a lead without pulling.

A puppy should get used to wearing a collar as soon as it has settled in its new home. When the puppy is used to wearing a collar you can put it on the lead and practise walking around the garden. The puppy should not be allowed on the streets or in the park, or any place where other dogs have been, until at least two weeks after its final vaccination. However, if you get the puppy used to walking on the lead, it should be fairly confident when it is ready to go further afield. Make sure the puppy walks alongside you, at your pace. If it gets away with pulling at this stage, you will have a big problem in a few months time when your St Bernard puppy will be quite capable of taking *you* for a walk or even run! It is important that the puppy

gets used to traffic and people while it is still young and easy to manage. To begin
with, take your puppy for a walk in a built-up area, but make sure it is a fairly quiet
place, particularly if you live in the country and the pup has never seen or heard
traffic. Give it time to get used to the new surroundings, and then gradually
encourage it to walk to heel. If the puppy tries to pull, give it a sharp tug back to
your side; you may need to use a choke-chain to get it to respond. As a puppy, it will
be easy to check, but this will become increasingly difficult as it gets bigger and
stronger, so the sooner your puppy learns this lesson, the better. Remember to
remove the choke-chain after training; if it is left on it could get caught up on any
obstacle, and prove very hazardous.

The next step is to teach your puppy to sit – but only on command. You will need
to push its rear down, telling it to "sit" at the same time. However, if you intend to
show your dog, you must be careful that it does not only associate a push on the rear
with sitting, as some judges press the rear to feel for strength of hindquarters. Teach
your puppy to lie down by pulling its front legs into the down position from the
sitting, and use the command "down", pointing downwards at the same time. When
your puppy understands these basic commands, teach it to stay. We always teach our
puppies this command at a very early stage. Most will understand it at eight to ten
weeks, when they are ready to go to their new homes. This basic command is
extremely useful: it stops a puppy racing towards the door ahead of you and tripping
you up; and if, by any chance, it is parted from you it could also stop it running
across a road. The easiest way to teach this command is to face the puppy, and then
gently, but firmly, hold it in the sit position. Then gradually start to back away,
saying "stay", and holding your hand towards the puppy, palm first, so that it has a
hand signal and a vocal command to back it up. Whenever it responds well to your
commands, give plenty of praise, and a titbit as a reward, if you like, and your puppy
will soon learn. Most dogs learn to come when you call them, as they all seek
attention. Command your puppy by using its name – which it should learn as soon as
it arrives in its new home – and saying "come". If the puppy tries to ignore you,
persevere with the command until it does; it must learn that you are the master. Do
not let your dog run loose, away from home, until you are confident that it will come
back to you. And no matter how well trained it is, do not let it loose near roads or
railways – and never let a nervous dog loose. You can never predict how a dog will
react to a sudden noise or disturbance, and you should never expose it to possible
dangers.

If you have purchased an older dog that is badly behaved or untrained, you will
need to embark on a rigorous training programme to try to correct its faults. Use a
choke chain, and when the dog pulls, give it a sharp pull to your side. Be careful to

put the choke chain on the right way so that it will release immediately, with the ring running freely, otherwise you could choke the dog. If the dog fails to respond to a choke chain, try using a head halter. This, as its name implies, is fitted round the dog's muzzle, and it will bring even the strongest St Bernard under control. You will probably have to put up with an initial 'bucking bronco' session, but when the dog realises that you have the upper hand and it can no longer get its own way by sheer force, it will submit to your control. It does not take a dog long to realise that where its head goes, the rest of its body must follow! In severe cases of pulling, you can try a halti, which is the trade name for the halter devised by Dr Roger Mugford. When the dog is wearing this, it cannot use its shoulders and body to pull against you. Eventually the dog will come to believe that you are stronger than it is. Then, if you wish, you can use the halti in conjunction with a choke chain. Hopefully the result will be that you can control the dog without the halti, even if it is only within the restrictions of the show ring.

It is a good idea to enrol your dog in a training class. There is usually a club in most areas, and the Kennel Club can provide a list of addresses. This will get your St Bernard used to being with dogs of all sizes, as well as teaching you how to handle your dog and teach it basic obedience. If you get on well, you can graduate to more advanced obedience and teach your dog retrieving, scent discrimination and walking to heel without a lead. You may wish to take part in obedience competitions, although, unfortunately, very few people in England train St Bernards to this level. However, in America many Saints hold obedience awards, and we have seen excellent team demonstrations from the St Bernard clubs in Holland, Italy and Switzerland. A few enthusiasts have trained their St Bernards to compete in Agility in other countries, but you need to join a club to do this, and obviously a lighter dog has the advantage over the heavily built St Bernard.

If you intend to show your dog you will already be half-way there if it walks well with you, but it will also need to be trained to stand. You can only do this with patience, putting the dog in a show position with its feet correctly placed, and commanding it to "stand". After the dog has kept the position for a reasonable time, give plenty of praise. Ask a friend to look at its teeth, firstly with its mouth closed so that its bite can be seen, and then opening the mouth to check its dentition. A show dog must get used to being handled all over, and again, you should enlist the help of a friend, so it becomes confident with different people and will not mind a judge going over it in the show ring. There are training clubs which specialise in ringcraft, and it is well worth joining one of these. Both obedience and ringcraft classes have experienced instructors who can train you and your dog to work as a team, which is the essential ingredient when you enter any kind of competition.

Chapter Four

GROOMING AND BATHING

There is very little grooming required to keep a short-haired St Bernard in top class condition. Regular brushing with a wire brush is usually quite adequate, although when a dog is casting its coat, you will need to use a fairly fine-toothed steel comb. This is the only time when a short-haired can look untidy. The dead coat can become quite tufty if it is not removed.

The long-haired St Bernard needs far more time and attention. The heavy feathering on the tail and back legs needs regular grooming, and so does the chest and shoulders. Small mats of hair can form under the armpits and behind the ears, and so these areas will also require special attention. However, a regular comb-through should keep the coat in good condition; the coat only mats if it is left unattended for long periods. We have discovered that textures of coats do vary, and some need much more attention than others. If a coat gets tangled, the best solution is to buy a dematting comb, and these are available from any good pet shop, or from a trade stand at one of the major shows. A dematting comb is a comb with blade edges that cut through the mat, enabling the animal to be groomed without causing it too much distress.

Heavily feathered ears need tidying up with a trimming comb, or the surplus hair can be plucked by hand with a dampened thumb and forefinger. The inner side of the ears can also be trimmed, and any surplus hair can be removed. Heavily feathered

St Bernards are often groomed on the table in the U.S.A.

ears are much more likely to cause trouble – getting dirty, or infections starting up – but we have found that they keep much healthier if the air is allowed to get through to them. Ears should be cleaned out at least once a week. This can be done with a piece of cotton-wool, which should be gently wiped round the inside of the ear. If the ears have any excessive discharge, veterinary treatment should be sought, as longterm ear infections are very difficult to eradicate.

The fur between the toes often needs attention. All tufts between the toes should be removed, and the feet should be trimmed up neatly. We have found that if you use trimming scissors, and cut against the hair, this has the best effect. Trimming scissors can also be used to tidy up the back of the hindlegs below the hock. The long fur on the back of the front legs should be combed out neatly – it should never be trimmed. Toe nails on dogs with correct feet rarely need trimming, providing that they are exercised on hard ground, which will wear them down. However, if your Saint's claws do grow long, they should be cut just below the quick – this is the pink fleshy bit inside the claw close to the toe. If you catch the quick, it will bleed and it is painful for the dog. It could also become infected. The front dewclaws should be trimmed regularly, although they do not tend to curl round as much as the back ones. To conform to the Breed Standard the dewclaws on the hindlegs should have been removed soon after birth. A few breeders also remove the front dewclaws, but this is not considered to be essential, although it does give a cleaner line to the front legs.

It is important to keep a St Bernard's eyes clean. They should be wiped with clean cotton-wool, either dampened with clean water or cold tea. If the eyes weep regularly, seek veterinary advice in case the dog is suffering from entropion. This is a condition where the eyelids turn inwards, and it will need corrective surgery otherwise the eye itself could be damaged. Entropion is hereditary, and it is much more likely to occur in the heavier-wrinkled dogs.

In the U.S.A. it is quite common to train your puppy to stand on a table to be groomed. Grooming tables with full-sized Saints standing on them are a common sight at the shows in America. This idea has never been adopted in Europe, although it is probably easier to groom at arm level, rather than having to bend over the dog, or go down on your hands and knees. If a puppy is trained to a grooming table from the start, it jumps on to it automatically, and is quite happy to stand there for the duration of the grooming session.

BATHING

Bathing a St Bernard for the first time may seem like an horrendous task to a newcomer to the breed. If you are showing your Saint, you will need to bath it more regularly – after all, it is a beauty show you are competing in. However, all dogs, including pets, need to be kept fresh and sweet-smelling, and so it is a job you will need to take on at some stage! If you try to bath your Saint in an upstairs bathroom, you will be giving yourself additional problems. It is relatively easy to persuade a dog to climb upstairs, but coming downstairs may be an entirely different matter. Unless a dog has been trained as a puppy to negotiate stairs, it will either be terrified and refuse to budge, or it will rush at them – and this could result in a fall. It is therefore preferable to use a downstairs bathroom, if possible, or use an old fashioned tin-bath in the garden. Obviously, you must choose a warm day if you are planning to bath outside. If you are bathing in the house, make sure all the doors to other rooms are shut. If, by any chance, your Saint makes a bid for freedom, you don't want to end up with a soggy dog jumping on your bed!

The bath should be filled with about four inches of warm water. The dog should be lifted in, back end first, followed by the front. If possible, try to encourage the dog to sit or lie down in the water. Then, using a jug or sponge, soak it all over and apply your dog shampoo, making a nice lather. Do not let the soap or water go in the eyes or into the ears. Once you are satisfied that the dog is covered all over with soapy lather, let the water out of the bath and start the rinsing. This can be done by either using a spray attachment to the bath, or with jugs of warm water. When the dog has

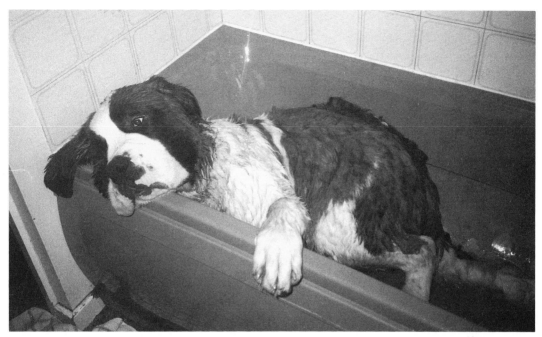

Bathing a St Bernard should not cause any problems if you follow the correct procedure.

been thoroughly rinsed, help it to get out of the bath, and then dry it with a towel. No doubt, the dog will give itself a good shake to get rid of the excess water – so be prepared to stand back! If the weather is warm you can let the dog run free in the garden in the sun. If the weather is cool or it is being prepared for a show, then dry the dog with a hair-dryer, grooming at the same time with a comb to remove any loose fur. You may by now find that you are wetter than the dog, so it may be advisable to have spare clothes readily available.

If, by any chance, you are now marooned upstairs with a clean, dry dog that won't come down, put a collar on the dog – not a choke chain – but make sure it is tight enough so that the dog cannot slip it. Hopefully, you can enlist the help of someone else, and the strongest person can go backwards down the stairs, holding the dog by its collar in one hand and holding the banister with the other. This should prevent the dog from sending you flying backwards. The other helper can go behind the dog and give it a push if it tries to dig its heels in. As you near the bottom of the stairs, be on your guard, as the dog may try and make a jump for it. Some Saints go up and down stairs quite happily on their own, but if they do not like a bath, they may shoot past the bathroom door, and it may take some persuading to get the dog to co-operate. However, if a dog is trained at an early stage to accept its bath, you should not have any problems.

Chapter Five

THE BREED STANDARD

Every judge, exhibitor, and breeder is governed by the Breed Standard. This lays down exactly what the breed should be in terms of physical make-up and temperament. It is the dogs that conform most closely to the Breed Standard that will be the most successful in the show ring, and it follows that these will be the specimens that are most likely to produce future generations of the breed. Therefore, the importance of the Breed Standard should never be underestimated: it is the cornerstone for every breed, and it shapes the future well-being of that breed.

In the case of the St Bernard the waters are muddied by the controversy that exists between the English Breed Standard and the American/continental Breed Standards. In essence, the American and continental Standards follow very similar lines, but Britain prefers to stand in isolation. The English Standard is very brief in terms of volume, and it does not appear to differ radically from the Breed Standard drawn up in the St Bernard's country of origin. However, it is the interpretation which differs, and this results in an English-type St Bernard, which would not be successful in show rings in America and on the continent. Equally, the American and continental types are not highly rated in Britain.

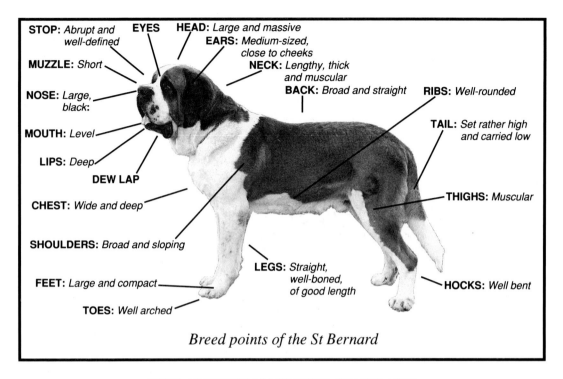

STOP: *Abrupt and well-defined*

EYES

HEAD: *Large and massive*

EARS: *Medium-sized, close to cheeks*

MUZZLE: *Short*

NECK: *Lengthy, thick and muscular*

NOSE: *Large, black:*

BACK: *Broad and straight*

RIBS: *Well-rounded*

MOUTH: *Level*

TAIL: *Set rather high and carried low*

LIPS: *Deep*

DEW LAP

CHEST: *Wide and deep*

THIGHS: *Muscular*

SHOULDERS: *Broad and sloping*

LEGS: *Straight, well-boned, of good length*

FEET: *Large and compact*

HOCKS: *Well bent*

TOES: *Well arched*

Breed points of the St Bernard

THE AMERICAN BREED STANDARD

SHORT-HAIRED

GENERAL Powerful, proportionately tall figure, strong and muscular in every part, with powerful head and most intelligent expression. In dogs with a dark mask the expression appears more stern, but never ill-natured.

HEAD Like the whole body, very powerful and imposing. The massive skull is wide, slightly arched and the sides slope in a gentle curve into the very strongly developed high cheek bones. Occiput only moderately developed. The supra-orbital ridge is very strongly developed and forms nearly a right angle with the horizontal axis of the head. Deeply embedded between the eyes and starting at the root of the muzzle, a furrow runs over the whole skull. It is strongly marked in the first half, gradually disappearing toward the base of the occiput. The lines at the sides of the head diverge considerably from the outer corner of the eyes toward the back of the head. The skin of the forehead, above the eyes, forms rather noticeable wrinkles, more or less pronounced, which converge toward the furrow. Especially when the dog is in action, the wrinkles are more visible without in the least giving the impression of morosity. Too strongly developed wrinkles are not desired. The slope from the skull to the muzzle is sudden and rather steep. The muzzle is short, does not taper, and the vertical depth at the root of the muzzle must be greater than the length of the muzzle. The bridge of the muzzle is not arched, but straight; in some dogs, occasionally, slightly broken. A rather wide, well marked, shallow furrow runs from the root of the muzzle over the entire bridge of the muzzle to the nose. The flews of the upper jaw are strongly developed, not sharply cut, but turning in a beautiful curve into the lower edge, and slightly overhanging. The flews of the lower jaw must not be deeply pendent. The teeth should be sound and strong and should meet in either a scissors or an even bite; the scissors bite being preferable. The undershot bite, although sometimes found with good specimens is not desirable. The overshot bite is a fault. A black roof to the mouth is desirable.

NOSE (Schwamm): Very substantial, broad with wide open nostrils and like the lips, always black.

EARS Of medium size, rather high set, with very strongly developed burr (Muschel) at base. They stand slightly away from the head at base, then drop with a sharp bend to the side and cling to the head without a turn. The flap is tender and forms a rounded triangle, slightly elongated toward the point, the front edge lying firmly to the head, whereas the back edge may stand somewhat away from the head, especially when the dog is at attention. Lightly set ears, which at the base immediately cling to the head, give it an oval and too little marked exterior, whereas a strongly developed base gives the skull a squarer, broader and much more expressive appearance.

EYES Set more to the front than the sides, are of medium size, dark brown, with intelligent, friendly expression, set moderately deep. The lower eyelids, as a rule, do not close completely and, if that is the case, form an angular wrinkle toward the inner corner of the eye. Eyelids which are too deeply pendent and show conspicuously the lachrimal glands, or a very red, thick hair, and eyes that are too light are objectionable.

NECK Set high, very strong and in action is carried erect. Otherwise horizontally or slightly downward. The junction of head and neck is distinctly marked by an indentation. The nape of the neck is very muscular and rounded at the sides which makes the neck appear rather short. The dewlap of the throat and neck is well pronounced; too strong development, however, is not desirable.

The American type: Ch. Subira's The General v Boris. Owned by William Buell and Sandra Rodrigo.

SHOULDERS Sloping, broad, very muscular, powerful. Withers strongly pronounced.

CHEST Very well arched, moderately deep, not reaching below the elbows.

BACK Very broad, perfectly straight as far as the haunches, from there gently sloping to the rump, and merging imperceptibly into the root of the tail.

HINDQUARTERS Well-developed. Legs very muscular.

BELLY Distinctly set off from the very powerful loin section, only little drawn up.

TAIL Starting broad and powerful directly from the rump is long, very heavy, ending in a powerful tip. In repose it hangs straight down, turning gently upward in the lower third only, which is not considered a fault. In a great many specimens the tail is carried with the end slightly bent and therefore hangs down in the shape of an 'f'. In action all dogs carry the tail more or less turned upward. However, it may not

The Continental type: Int. Sw.& Nor. Ch. Bernegarden's All Alone.

be carried too erect or by any means rolled over the back. A slightly curling of the tip is sooner admissible.

FOREARMS Very powerful and extraordinarily muscular.

FORELEGS Straight, strong.

HIND LEGS Hocks of moderate angulation. Dewclaws are not desired; if present they must not obstruct gait.

FEET Broad, with strong toes, moderately closed, and with rather high knuckles. The so-called dewclaws, which sometimes occur on the inside of the hind legs, are imperfectly developed toes. They are of no use to the dog and are not taken into consideration in judging. They may be removed by surgery.

COAT Very dense, short-haired (stockhaarig), lying smooth, tough, without, however, feeling rough to the touch. The thighs are slightly bushy. The tail at the root has longer and denser hair which gradually becomes shorter toward the tip. The tail appears bushy, not forming a flag.

COLOR White with red, or red with white, the red in its various shades; brindle patches with white markings. The colors red and brown-yellow are of entirely equal value. Necessary markings are: white chest, feet and tip of tail, noseband, collar or spot on the nape; the latter and blaze are very desirable. Never of one color or without white. Faults are all other colors, except the favourite dark shadings on the head (mask) and ears. One distinguishes between mantle and splash-coated dogs.

HEIGHT AT SHOULDER The dog should be $27\frac{1}{2}$ inches minimum, the bitches $25\frac{1}{2}$ inches. Female animals are of finer, more delicate build.

FAULTS All deviations from the Standard, as for instance a sway back, hocks that are bent too much, straight hindquarters, upward growing hair in spaces between the toes, out at elbows, cow hocks, or weak pasterns.

LONG-HAIRED

The long-haired type completely resembles the short-haired type except for the coat which is not short-haired (stockhaarig) but of medium length plain to slightly wavy, never rolled or curly and not shaggy either. Usually, on the back, especially from the region of the haunches to the rump, the hair is more wavy – a condition, by the way, that is lightly indicated in the short-haired dogs. The tail is bushy with dense hair of moderate length. Rolled or curly hair on the tail is not desirable. A tail with parted hair, or a flag tail, is faulty. Face and ears are covered with short and soft hair; longer hair at the base of the ear is permissible. Forelegs only slightly feathered; thighs very bushy.

Reproduced by kind permission of he American Kennel Club.

THE ENGLISH BREED STANDARD

GENERAL APPEARANCE Well proportioned and of great substance.

CHARACTERISTICS: Distinctly marked, large-sized, mountain-rescue dog.

The British type: Ch. Swindridge Geraldine.

TEMPERAMENT: Steady, kindly, intelligent, courageous, trustworthy and benevolent.

HEAD AND SKULL: Large, massive circumference of skull being rather more than double its length. Muzzle short, full in front of eye and square at nose end. Cheeks flat, great depth from eye to lower jaw. Lips deep but not too pendulous. From nose to stop perfectly straight and broad. Stop somewhat abrupt and well defined. Skull broad, slightly rounded at top, with fairly prominent brow. Nose large and black with well developed nostrils.

EYES: Of medium size, neither deep set nor prominent, eyelids should be reasonably tight, without any excessive haw. Dark in colour and not staring. There should be no excessive loose wrinkle on brow to detract from a healthy eye.

EARS: Medium size, lying close to cheeks, not heavily feathered.

MOUTH: Jaws strong, with a perfect, regular and complete scissor bite, i.e. upper teeth closely overlapping lower teeth and set square to the jaws.

NECK: Long, thick, muscular, slightly arched, dewlap well developed.

FOREQUARTERS: Shoulders broad and sloping, well up at withers. Legs straight, strong in bone, of good length.

BODY: Back broad, straight, ribs well rounded. Loin wide, very muscular. Chest wide and deep, but never projecting below elbows.
HINDQUARTERS: Legs heavy in bone, hocks well bent, thighs very muscular.

FEET: Large, compact with well arched toes. Dewclaws removed.

TAIL: Set on rather high, carried low when in repose, when excited or in motion should not curl over back.

GAIT/MOVEMENT: Easy extension, unhurried or smooth, capable of covering difficult terrain.

COAT: In Roughs dense and flat, rather fuller round neck, thighs and tail well feathered. In Smooths, close and hound-like, slight feathering on thighs and tail.

COLOUR: Orange, mahogany-brindle, red-brindle, white patches on body of any above named colours. Markings: white muzzle, white blaze on face, white collar, white chest, white forelegs, feet and end of tail, black shadings on face and ears.

SIZE: Taller the better, provided symmetry is maintained.

FAULTS: Any departure from the foregoing points should be considered a fault and the seriousness with which the fault should be regarded should be in exact proportion to the degree.

NOTE: Male animals should have two apparently normal testicles fully descended into the scrotum.
Reproduced by kind permission of the English Kennel Club.

ANALYSIS OF THE BREED STANDARD

GENERAL APPEARANCE

The general comments of the American/continental Breed Standards are equally applicable to the English Breed Standard; it is the head which causes the most controversy. Anyone outside Britain might describe the typical English head as resembling a Bloodhound, with heavy wrinkle, long droopy lips, saggy eyes showing excessive haw, and little or no stop. Of course, many St Bernard heads are not so exaggerated and today these comments are not really justified. In fact, the English Breed Standard describing the eye has been altered in recent years to try to eradicate the hereditary conditions entropion (eyelids turning in, which can cause ulceration of the eye itself, and in extreme cases blindness) and ectropion (eyelids too open and turning out). Admittedly, the heavy wrinkled head was the chief desire of most judges in the fifties and early sixties, and little else was of any importance in the United Kingdom. So long as a dog had a good head, it did not matter whether or not it had anything else going for it. The old English Breed Standard gave a points system, of which 40 were allocated for the head. However, the dog's overall appearance and its movement count for much more today, although little stop and excessive lips are still acceptable to some St Bernard enthusiasts. If you were to look round a ring full of St Bernards in England, at present, there are many different types, and this is very confusing to the newcomer. In the U.S.A. and the rest of Europe, the breed does not vary to the same extent. A dog with a good continental type head can gain its Championship title in Europe or America, whereas a dog with an English-type head has no hope of winning honours in the rest of Europe, or the U.S.A. Some of the Australian St Bernards are more akin to the English type, because originally Australia could only import through England.

TEMPERAMENT

The St Bernard should have, and usually does have, a stable, loving and loyal temperament. It should be completely trustworthy with the family, but it should be prepared to guard its owners in times of danger.

HEAD

The Americans and continentals prefer a higher ear-set; the preference is for a considerably lower ear-set in Britain. The continentals like a St Bernard head to be fairly flat between the ears, and it must have a distinct stop. The head of the American St Bernard is slightly more rounded.

A typical American head: Ch. Vieledanke Hello Dolly. Owned and bred by Carmelo and Cheryl Zappala.

A typical British Head: Ch. Swindridge Mathew.

A typical Continental head: Int.Ch. Sankt Cardis Anton

EYES

The eye colouring of the English St Bernard is usually good, being very dark, but lighter eyes are frequently found elsewhere. When the lighter eye blends in with the coat, it does not detract from the general appearance, but a very light eye in a dark-coloured dog looks atrocious, and often gives a very hard expression. This is quite at odds with the benevolent expression which should be typical of the breed.

MOUTH

The correct even bite is usually found in the English Saint, whereas the scissor bite with the under jaw fitting over the upper jaw has always been frowned upon in

England, although it should be acceptable according to the Breed Standard. We have seen many more dogs with this bite in other countries, and it does give a stronger appearance to the muzzle. There are also a considerable number of undershot mouths, i.e. the lower jaw not meeting the upper jaw, in the foreign show ring. The overshot bite is seldom seen. Long lips and dewlaps are preferred in the United Kingdom, while elsewhere the strong square muzzle is deep, without the flews being too pendulous.

NECK

The neck is very important in contributing to the impression of nobility in the breed. A neck that is too short makes the dog look as though its head is just stuck on the body. A well arched neck gives the correct, proud appearance.

BODY

Most American and Scandinavian Saint Bernards, although sometimes shorter, are thicker-set than the English type with heavier chests and well rounded ribs. The continentals are similar in build to the English Saint. Many English St Bernards can be faulted for having a narrow chest, with both front legs almost looking as though they were emerging from one hole. Slab sides, i.e. flat ribs, is another common fault, which can appear even more pronounced in some of the taller dogs. On the plus side, the English St Bernard has the heaviest bone of any in the world, and is among the biggest. There are also some very large dogs in Italy, Germany and Holland.

FOREQUARTERS AND HINDQUARTERS

In recent years much more emphasis has been placed on the complete dog. The aim is for a dog to look in proportion with four legs squarely placed. The hind legs should be quite well angulated, but not exaggerated or giving a sloping topline – the back should be straight. Dewclaws are generally removed from the back legs. Some breeders also remove them from the front legs, believing that the front legs have a neater outline without them.

FEET

All the Breed Standards require cat-like feet, i.e. well arched toes, not appearing too open or splayed, although the latter is a fairly common fault.

TAIL

In the long-haired variety the tail should hang down, almost like a fox's brush. The short-haired's tail should hang in the same way, the only difference is that it does not have any feathering. There is no ruling on the amount of feathering on a long-haired tail, but a heavily feathered one always looks nice. A short-haired tail should have short thick fur, with no hanging feathers. The tail may have a small kink at the end, but the tip must reach down at least as far as the hocks, otherwise it appears too short. A common fault in British dogs is for the tail to be carried high over the back when in action, known as a gay tail. The tail should not curl into a double ring, but this fault is rarely seen today. If the tail is set too high, it is rarely carried correctly.

GAIT/MOVEMENT
A St Bernard should move squarely, neither too wide, nor appearing bandy-legged or pin-toed. The legs should move parallel to each other. The hocks should not touch, or turn in, which is termed 'cow hocked'. The stifles should not appear to turn in, although this, and cow hocks, are fairly common faults in the show ring. A St Bernard must not move with a shuffling action; it must look strong and positive, as though it was capable of carrying out a day's work in the snow. Back legs should follow the same parallel line of the front, and movement should appear even and free-flowing.

COAT
In the short-haired variety the coat should be dense all over. The long-haired should have heavy feathering on the chest, neck, and back of hind legs, and a bushy tail.

COLOUR
The St Bernard in the U.K. is usually darker in colour than those of other countries, and it has much heavier black shadings. There are also different views on colouring. Many of the English breeders and exhibitors and judges like the freckling, which is sometimes quite heavy on the white of the muzzle and legs of their dogs. This flecking is frowned upon elsewhere, and the white markings are usually completely clean. The British St Bernard can have a much narrower blaze, and less white on the muzzle. A mantle coat is generally sought after throughout Europe. Splash coats are seen more often in Scandinavia and America.

SIZE
The American Breed Standard stipulates a minimum size of $27\frac{1}{2}$ inches at the shoulder for dogs, and $25\frac{1}{2}$ inches for bitches. The old British Standard used to give a minimum of 29 inches and 27 inches respectively, but now it merely states the taller the better, provided symmetry is maintained, and most males dogs are usually much bigger than this minimum requirement.

Chapter Six

THE ST BERNARD IN THE UNITED KINGDOM

The first recorded St Bernard to arrive in England was a dog called Lionn, imported from the Hospice in Switzerland in 1815, and brought to Leasowe Castle, near Birkenhead, in 1815. Many more were subsequently imported, mainly from the Hospice. Queen Victoria owned two St Bernards in the 1840s, and the Royal connection did much to advance the popularity of the breed, particularly among the nobility. The first official dog shows started in 1862, and it was around this time that the Reverend Cumming Macdonna developed an interest in the Mount Saint Bernhard Dog, as it was then known, and imported many good dogs from Switzerland. The most famous of these was Tell, sired by Hero ex Diane and bred in Berne by Herr Schindler, who was never beaten in the show ring. Macdonna then imported Hedwig, and bred Alp from him, who was later exported to the U.S.A. He also imported dogs from the renowned Herr Schumacher, and from the Hospice. A St Bernard called Hope was shown by the Prince of Wales and won prizes at Crystal Palace. Other important imports were Leo, owned by Sir Charles Isham, and Thor, imported by Mr J. H. Murchison and purchased from Herr Schumacher. Mr Fred Gresham also established a very successful kennel. The most famous descendants of these early imports were Bayard, Plinlimmon and Sir Bedivere. By the late 1870s the St Bernard was the favourite large-size companion dog in England. There were approximately seventy entries at both the Crystal Palace show in 1879 and the

Sir Bedivere was one of the first British prize-winners, later sold to the U.S.A.

Alexandra Palace show in the same year. The idea of forming a St Bernard Club was first conceived by the Reverend Arthur Carter in December 1881 at Alexandra Palace, and it was officially formed in February 1882. At this time, the St Bernard Club was the only specialist breed club to hold its own shows. It presented prizes to show committees, and donated two 100 guineas Challenge Cups, which became much sought after in the breed. Bayard won a Challenge Cup twice, and Plinlimmon won one three times. Today, these two trophies are owned by the English St Bernard Club. The first St Bernard shows held from 1882 onwards attracted entries of 252, 264, 247 and 303 over the first four years. Plinlimmon won the 1884 show – he stood 33 inches at the shoulder and weighed 223 pounds. Sir Bedivere was of the same impressive proportions, and was sold to America for £1300. The Swiss were afraid that the English would attempt to dominate them when it came to determining the future type of the Swiss St Bernard, and the Swiss Kennel Club was formed for its protection. Dr Th. Kunzli, who had between seventy and a hundred Saints in his kennel in Switzerland, attended an International Congress in Brussels with Dr Siegmund and Swiss delegates, to defend the Swiss Standard against the English in 1886. No agreement was reached until 1887, when discussions were held over a

Mrs Staines and her Abbotspass celebrities, Romeo, Macbeth, Brownie, Ben and Benedick.

three-day period from June 3rd to June 6th at the International show at Zurich. The Swiss Standard was accepted by all countries except England. Even Scotland was prepared to accept the International Standard, but England remained adamant in its isolation.

The St Bernard Club stated that its principal object was to encourage the breeding of St Bernard dogs of a certain recognised type and to stimulate popular interest in these only, to the exclusion of others of a different and objectionable character. To do this, the club undertook to define the type and urge the adoption of this type on breeders, exhibitors, judges, dog show committees and others as the only Breed Standard by which St Bernards should be judged. The National St Bernard Club was founded in 1899, mainly at the instigation of Dr Inman, who with Mr C. Walmsley owned the Bowden kennel. This club was the direct outcome of a Liverpool and Northern Counties St Bernard Club begun by Messrs Foster and Bowley and others in 1893. It is interesting to note that the 1953 Handbook of the English St Bernard Club gives the date of its foundation as 1891 on its front cover.

However, during this period there was excessive indiscriminate breeding both in England and in Switzerland to supply the English demand for St Bernards, and this craze, coupled with the desire to own the biggest St Bernard, contributed to the decline of the breed. The Bowden kennels tried to concentrate on soundness as well as type, and they achieved considerable success with such dogs as: Tannhauser, who won sixteen Challenge Certificates between 1901 and 1905; Viola, winner of fourteen Challenge Certificates; The King's Son, a fine smooth; and The Viking. Then, in 1912, Ch. The Pride of Sussex won Best in Show at Crufts and

Birmingham. Mr and Mrs J. Redwood formed their Pearl kennel from Bowden stock, and they managed to keep it going through the First World War. Mr Redwood became secretary of the English St Bernard Club when it started up after the war, and his wife carried on breeding St Bernards long after his death in 1932.

Ch. Bernardo was one of the foundation dogs of the Abbotspass kennels, owned by Mrs Staines. Bernardo and his sister Nerissa were bred by Mr Chasty out of Ch. The King's Daughter and Ch. Benedict Pearl. Mrs Staines imported Swiss dogs and achieved much success. Ch. Abbotspass Macbeth, Ch. Abbotspass Friar, Ch. Abbotspass Portia, Ch. Abbotspass Benedick and Ch. Abbotspass Romeo are just a few of her better known dogs. Ch. Abbotspass Friar was bought by Mr Brearley and Mr Mellor, and he was said to be the only full-grown sire to be sold by Mrs Staines. She turned down an offer of £2,000 for Romeo, and when Romeo died at seven years old he was stuffed to preserve his image for posterity. The Misses Pratt from Scotland also imported Swiss stock. They mated their imported bitch Emira Flora to Moorgate Masterpiece and they produced Ch. Berndean Ailza and Ch. Mhora in 1932, and a year later a repeat mating produced Ch. The Marquis of Wetterhorn and Ch. Berndean Roderick. Ch. Berndean Invader was still very much in evidence on the pedigrees when we came into the breed. Mrs Staines gave the two magnificent Abbotspass trophies to the English St Bernard Club. She also donated two trophies to Crufts – one of these was stolen, and the other is awarded to the Best of Breed in Pyrenean Mountain Dogs. The St Bernard clubs have appealed for the return of the stolen cup, but to no avail.

Mrs Briggs of the Beldene kennels, Mr Barton (Moorgate), Miss Watts (Clairvaux), Mr Brierley (Copleydene), Horace Mellor (Friezland), Dr and Mrs Cox (Priorslegh), Mrs Graydon Bradley (Boystown), Mr A. E. Thompson (Loundes) and Mr A. K. Gaunt (firstly Twokays, then Cornagarth) were the other well-known names of the time. It was these people who kept the breed going during the Second World War. Mrs Graydon Bradley lived at Dover and suffered many losses due to air raids; she came back after the war and made Boystown Cavalier a Champion in 1951. We had one of the last of her dogs, Boystown Roy.

Ken Gaunt is recorded as a member of the English St Bernard Club in 1931, and he and his wife Kathleen started their kennels from some of the best stock of the time. They bought Yew Tree St Christopher from Mrs Connie Walker, and this dog, born in 1943, became the first post-war Champion in 1947. A year later Ken made Cornagarth Wendy of Flossmere a Champion. She was a beautiful bitch who won everywhere she went, but unfortunately she could not be used for breeding. Ch. Yew Tree St Christopher went on to sire eleven Champions, only one of which was bred by Cornagarth – Ch. Cornagarth Colonel. This smooth coat won Best of Breed at

Pat Muggleton with Ch. Christcon St Jeremy, Ken Gaunt with Ch. Christcon St Iris.

Crufts in 1952. However, Ken Gaunt's policy of having the pick of the litter in lieu of the stud fee, and also buying any other puppies sired by his dog that he fancied, was most advantageous. He made up another four Champions, sired by Ch. Yew Tree St Christopher, in this way. Ch. Cornagarth Culzean Nero, bred by Miss Bryce from Glasgow, and Ch. Cornagarth Cornborrow St Oliver also carried St Christopher's line on to many future Cornagarth Champions, and all English-bred stock could probably trace its ancestry back to him. In 1950 Ken Gaunt was lucky enough to buy Marshall van Zwing Uri for a nominal figure. Marshall had already been imported from Switzerland. He was totally different from English dogs of the time, and show reports included such comments as "a complete break from English Standards". However, he was completely sound and did much to improve the overall soundness in the breed at a time when it was greatly needed. In the fifties, it was a common sight to see a cow-hocked dog, or one with terrible movement, winning a CC – although it would have the most beautiful head. At this time there was a scale of points in the Breed Standard, and 40 points were allocated for the head. In many people's eyes, judges included, nothing else but the head seemed to matter. Marshall stood out from the English-bred Saints, but he became a Champion, and produced just two Champion children – Ch. Cornagarth Thornebarton Jungfrau, bred by Mrs Slazenger, who changed her prefix to Durrowabbey when she moved to Eire; and

Enid Muggleton with Cornagarth Recorder of Bernmont, Pat with Bernmont Fiona.
Ch. Cornagarth Guardsman. However, many Cornagarth/Durrowabbey stock
descended from Jungfrau. Ken Gaunt used to send the puppies to Mrs Slazenger to
be reared; he would then campaign them in the show ring as adults, and most of
them became Champions. The Muggletons' Bernmont prefix was established in

Eng. & Ir. Ch. Burtonswood Bossy Boots: Crufts Supreme Champion 1974.
Owned and bred by Miss Marjorie Hindes.

1950, and the kennel was lucky enough to buy Cornagarth Recorder of Bernmont, a son of Marshall. He was the sire of John and Mary Harpham's first St Bernard, and also their first Champion – Ch. Bernmont Felicity. They started the Whaplode kennel, but then had a break of ten years, and it was the Cornagarths that dominated the show scene in the fifties and sixties.

Another kennel of note at this time was the Peldartor Kennel of Mrs R. L. Walker, assisted by her son Gilbert, who always handled the dogs. Mrs Walker bought Cornagarth Dawn in 1947, and later Cornagarth Belinda. Dawn was mated to Beldene Mickado, and she produced littermates: Ch. Carol of Peldartor, a rough, and Ch. Colossus of Peldartor, a smooth. She also bought St Dominic of Brenchley – which she made a Champion – and Charnwood Bruno from the monks of Mount St Bernard's Abbey in Charnwood Forest, Leicestershire. Bruno was by Beldene Ajax out of Monberno Belle. He was a tall dog with a beautiful head, and he also gained his title. Mrs Walker acquired the imported German bitch, Anka von der Deuke Schlense, who became a Champion. She mated Anka to Charnwood Bruno and produced a lovely litter of eight. She sold only one, and kept all the rest. The best known of these were Ch. Peldartor Rosseau and Ch. Peldartor Ranee. Several other Champions followed, but, other than through the lines of her first two stud dogs, little now remains from the Peldartors.

Miss Marjorie Hindes mated her first bitch, Cornagarth Coronet, to Ch. Peldartor Charnwood Bruno in 1955, and produced Ch. Prima Donna of Burtonswood. From this foundation, she bred many Burtonswood Champions. She only kept bitches at the beginning, and always used Cornagarth sires. Later on, however, she kept males and in 1970 she made Ch. Burtonswood Black Diamond a Champion. He won a total of six CCs, but greater things were to follow. In 1974 she won Best in Show at Crufts with Ch. Burtonswood Bossy Boots. He was home-bred by the German-bred dog Cornagarth Kuno von Birkenkopf and her bitch, Ch. Burtonswood Beloved. Kuno was one of a litter of six, bred in quarantine by a newcomer to the breed, Michael Gilbey. Mr Gilbey brought the bitch Gundi v Birkenkopf into the country in whelp to the Swiss dog Alex von Pava. The litter was reared in quarantine, and when Gundi had finished with her puppies she was returned to her native land. Mr Gilbey kept two pups, Ken Gaunt bought Kuno, and Daphne Ayckbourne gave Mr Gilbey an "open cheque" for the remaining three. Daphne was another breeder to emerge in the late forties, and Daphnedene Ramona, the foundation bitch of the Bernmont strain, came from her. She kept a small kennel, showing dogs on an occasional basis, until she bought the German-bred puppies. She made Daphnedene Karro von Birkenkopf a Champion and won two CCs with his brother, King. Ken Gaunt's Kuno never became a Champion himself, but he sired eleven Champions and is in the pedigree of most St Bernards in the U.K. today.

One of the more impressive sights at shows in the early fifties was the arrival of Mr W. D. Joslin, complete with his kennel manageress and a team of kennelmen, all immaculately turned out in white coats. Needless to say, his dogs were equally well presented – a point on which many dogs of the day failed – and some still do today! Mr Joslin made up four Champions: Ch. Snowbound Travellers Joy of St Olam and Ch. Snowbound Beau Cherie of St Olam, both bred by Mr Wilder of the Snowbound kennels – a wartime kennel that did not exhibit much; and Ch. St Olam Regent Prince and Ch. St Olam Sultan. Regent Prince won Best in Show at Leeds Championship Show in 1951, and Joslin turned down an offer of £2,300 from America for Beau Cherie, who won many CCs.

The only other breeder of any significance in these times was Mrs Connie Hutchings, formerly Mrs Walker of the Yew Trees. Connie started breeding again with Cornagarth Comet, mating her to a son of Ch. Yew Tree St Christopher – Ch. Cornagarth Culzean Nero. The resulting litter included Ch. Christcon St Anthony, who won ten CCs, and Ch. Christcon St Arline. A subsequent litter from Cornagarth Comet, sired by Cornagarth Durrowabbey St Patrick, produced the glorious Christcon St Iris. Mrs Hutchings, again, did not remain in the breed for long, and she sold all her stock in 1960 when she went to live in France, where her husband had bought a vineyard. Christcon St Iris, already a Champion, was purchased by Ken Gaunt, and Christcon St Jeremy – a son of Christcon St Barco and St Colliers

Clare Bradley with Ch. Monbardon Sir Jonathan (left) and Sir Jonathan of St Bury.

Genevieve – came to the Bernmonts. The Bernmont kennel also purchased Christcon St Rajar and Christcon St Olwyn, our first smooths, and Christcon Sonia of Solentvale – the Solentvales were one of the few lines with any Peldartor blood. Christcon St Jeremy already had two CCs at this stage, and we completed his title, also winning the CC at Crufts in 1962 when Ch. Christcon St Iris took Best of Breed. Miss Hindes bought Christcon St Olga, and she also gained her crown.

Mr W. F. Barazetti wrote and published a book on the breed in the mid-fifties. He was Swiss, and he could therefore translate much of the interesting information on the breed first-hand. While his book was most instructive, it was poorly printed and few copies have survived. Mr Barazetti bred two Champions: Ch. Cornagarth Bulldrummond of St Bury, a smooth born in 1946 out of St Marcuson and Copleydene St Lionetta; and Brownie of St Bury, who was out of a home-bred bitch and sired by Ch. Yew Tree St Christopher, and was campaigned by Barazetti to win his title.

There were only two English newcomers to the Saints scene in the sixties, and both had a liking for the continental type. Dr Una Westell of the Fernebrandons bred two Champions – Fernebrandon Achilles and Fernebrandon Agrippa – in her first litter. She had bought the Swiss-imported bitch, Brita von Salmegg, in partnership with Mrs Dixon. The sire was Ch. Christcon St Jeremy. Dr. Westell mated Ch. Garry of Bryneithin to Brita the following year. A son of this union was Westernisles Fernebrandon Brutus, owned by Mrs Fairbrother. When Albert de la Rie awarded him the CC and Best of Breed at the S.K.C., he described him as the best dog in

Europe. He was a large, sound dog with a good continental-type head. He won another CC and three reserve CCs, but along with many other good-looking continental-type dogs, he never gained his title.

Mrs Clare Bradley made Monbardon Sir Jonathan a Champion in 1960. He was used as the model for a beautiful coloured card by the well-known firm, Kaye Cards, and he was used as the model for the English St Bernard Club badge. Ken Gaunt owned his litter brother, Ch. Cornagarth Morbarden Sir Marcus – the dogs were a combination of Yew Tree St Christopher and Marshall van Zwing Uri bloodlines. Marcus sired nine Champions, including Ch. Cornagarth Moira and Ch. Cornagarth For Tops. For Tops, later exported to Japan along with several other Cornagarth Champions, was the double grandsire of Ch. Burtonswood Beloved, the mother of the renowned Bossy Boots. Ch. Monbardon St Jonathan sired Snowranger Saucy Sue, the dam of the lovely Ch. Snowranger Chloris, and Croesus, who were sired by Tello von Sauliamt, imported by Clare Bradley from Switzerland. Tello produced a much more active and long-lived dog than the current English type. Mrs Bradley, in partnership with Peter Hill, imported Bas von der Vrouwenpolder from Holland. Although he was the better dog and gained his English title, he did not produce such good quality stock as Tello, maybe because the two foreign lines were intermixed.

Ch. Bernmont Warlord was the top winner of his time. He was a massive dog of 37 inches, and he was also sound. He was shown on only ten occasions, and won nine CCs and Best of Breeds, and one reserve CC. He won the Working Group at Bath Championship Show in 1969; it was eighteen years since a St Bernard had won such a high honour, the last to do so being Ch. St Olam Regent Prince in 1951. Warlord also won Best of Breed at Crufts in 1971. He was sired by Bernmont Snowranger Statesman – a son of Saucy Sue who we acquired from Clare Bradley in lieu of a stud fee – out of our Ch. Christcon St Jeremy. Warlord's dam was Bernmont Carol, a daughter of Jeremy and Bernmont Sandra. Sandra was out of Bernmont Boystown Roy and Bernmont Melody. Melody was a great granddaughter of our first bitch, Daphnedene Ramona, and granddaughter of our first dog, Cornagarth Recorder of Bernmont. In general the breed was quite interbred at the turn of the decade, and the use of the imported Kuno von Birkenkopf did much to improve the stamina and soundness of the breed.

Two litter sisters, born in 1967, became Champions in 1971. They were by Ch. Cornagarth Koon out of Cornagarth Cordette: Cornagarth Marquisite was owned by Mrs Maureen Gwilliam of the Coatham prefix, and Cornagarth Mirabelle was owned by Mr Michael Braysher of the Braypass kennel. Mr Braysher also made up Ch. Burtonswood Big Time in the same year. Both Mrs Gwilliam and Mr Braysher are still active in the breed. The Coatham prefix is now jointly owned with

John Boulden with Ch. Middlepark Grand Monarque.   *Dalton.*

Maureen's husband, George. They bred and owned Ch. Coatham Starshine, Ch. Coatham Hermes and Ch. Coatham Suffragette. They also bred Hilary Taylor's two Champions: Coatham Worthy Commissioner and Coatham Commissioners Aide. They owned Ch. Be Elect of Burtonswood, who was the dam of Dennis Owen's Ch. Coatham Gin 'n Tonic. Her daughter, Denbow Miss Muffat, did a lot of winning. George Gwilliam campaigned Alpentire on Commission to his title, and their latest Champion is Dragonville Lord Snooty of Coatham, who won the Southern Club's Dog Of The Year competition in 1991. He was bred by Jean Frost, sired by the Gwilliam's dog, Coatham Ripe Harvest, out of a daughter of Ch. Pankraz von den drei Helmen of Bernmont. Mr Braysher's most famous dog was a son of Ch. Burtonswood Bossy Boots, his home-bred Ch. Baypass Sportsman. This was a dog with colossal front legs, although, unfortunately, he was not the best of movers. Other Braypass Champions were Burrill and Marina. Mr Braysher recently imported two Saints from the Opdyke kennels in America.

Ch. Lindenhall High Commissioner was the first Champion of Richard and Rachel Beaver's Lindenhall kennels. He also won more CCs than any of the other Lindenhall Champions that were to follow in the seventies. High Commissioner was one of five Champions in their first litter from Cornagarth Adelaide and Kuno. The others were Lindenhall High and Mighty, Highlight, High Commander and High Admiral, owned by D. Campbell. The best known of the others was Ch. Lindenhall Capability Brown, a smooth who won six CCs. Prior to his marriage to Rachel, Richard won two CCs with Gershwin Melody in the late sixties.

The stock from the German litter was spread all over the country by numerous new small kennels. John and Sheila Boulden, from Kent, bred their first litter from

John Harpham with Ch. Whaplode Ivanhoe, Ch. Whaplode Margaret, Ch. Whaplode King and Ch. Whaplode Desdemona. *Lincolnshire Free Press.*

Calpurnius of Andlyn and Plutopian Kent von Birkenkopf. Hugo, Humphrey and Harriet were retained, bearing the Middlepark name of their farm. John trained Hugo as a sheepdog, a task at which he was most proficient, showing that St Bernards can be extremely versatile if you have the time to train them for a specific job. Born in 1974, Hugo and Humphrey lived to be eleven and a half and twelve years old respectively. John now has another home-bred St Bernard trained to herd his sheep. When Middlepark Harriet was mated to Ch. Benem Sir Galahad, she produced their first home-bred Champion, Middlepark Prudence. They had previously been successful in the show ring with Ch. Burtonswood Black Duke. They have since made Prudence's son, Middlepark Grand Monarque a Champion, and are currently showing their smooth-coated bitch Middlepark Gabriella successfully.

John and Mary Harpham renewed their interest in the breed and bought two daughters of Ch. Cornagarth Stroller – Cornagarth Alma and Cornagarth Anna. Alma mated to Kuno gave them Ch. Whaplode Desdemona, and Anna was mated to a smooth-coated son of Kuno – Cornagarth Askan. From the resulting litter they retained a smooth, Whaplode Emperor, who won two CCs before his premature death. His litter brother, the rough-coated Ch. Whaplode Eros of Bernmont, won Best of Breed at Crufts in 1978. Emperor had two Champion sons: the smooth

Ch. Roddinghead Agent Kris of Knockespoch. Owned by Sue Roberts.

Dalton.

Ch. Topvalley Wogans Winner. Owned by Mrs Greta Topping.   *C. M. Cooke.*

Whaplode King and the rough Whaplode Ivanhoe. Ivanhoe was top dog 1978 and, as such, set the trend for his descendants. One of his most successful sons was Ch. Whaplode Unique, who was out of Whaplode Juliette. This dog was the breed recordholder of his time, top dog in 1981 and 1982 and top stud dog in 1983, 1984 and 1985. He won Best of Breed at Crufts in 1981, when Pat was judging. His full brother from a later litter was Ch. Whaplode My Lord, who was top dog in 1983 and top stud dog in 1988. Yet another top-winning offspring of Unique was Ch. Lucky Charm of Whaplode, bred by Sue Roberts out of Ch. Roddinghead Agent Kris of Knockespoch. Lucky Charm is still the breed recordholder, with a tally of twenty-five CCs. She was joint top dog in 1986. Ch. Bishopsway Moses of Whaplode, a son of My Lord, looked more like his twin. He won Best of Breed at Crufts in 1989 and 1990. The Whaplodes are now owned by John and Mary in partnership with their eldest daughter, Mrs Mary Pearl.

Greta Topping and her husband Eric started in the breed about the same time as the Harphams' return to it, also using Cornagarth stock. Their first Champion was the last Cornagarth bitch to be a Champion – Cornagarth Cara. Greta also had several Burtonswood dogs, including Ch. Burtonswood Be Fine. For many years her top winner, Ch. Topvalley Wogans Winner, tied with the Whaplodes for top dog. Wogans Winner was a son of Ch. Burtonswood Bossy Boots, and he won nineteen CCs and Best of Breed at Crufts in 1983. Topvalley Joanne was one of the youngest Champions and, although very small, she had quality, soundness and conformation. Other Champions to come from Greta's kennels were Ch. Topvalley Chardras, owned by E. N. Davies, Ch. Topvalley Carasel of Burtonswood, and Ch. Topvalley Anna. Ch. Topvalley Karl was her last Champion. He was a son of Wogan and won Best of Breed at Crufts in 1985. Although Mrs Topping no longer exhibits, she still keeps the St Bernard as a pet, and often assists at the club shows. Sadly, Eric Topping, who had always been a generous supporter of the English St Bernard Club, died two years ago.

Michael and Ann (Wensley) started the Swindridge St Bernards from Snowranger stock. Snowranger Your Delightful, a granddaughter of Ch. Snowranger Bas v.d.Vrouenpolder and Ch. Snowranger Chloris was put to the smooth son of Kuno, Cornagarth Askan. From this litter two bitches were retained: Swindridge Madam Acacia, a smooth, and Swindridge Madam Annaliese, a rough. A grand total of eleven Swindridge Champions are descended from these two bitches. A mating from Annaliese to the German-imported smooth, King vom St Klara Kloster, produced Ch. Swindridge Catherine, and Swindridge Charlotte, who went to Ireland and is the ancestor of many Irish Champions. Catherine was the only Champion sired by King. King and two bitches were imported from Germany by Ken Gaunt in the early seventies. Mrs Judy McMurray of the Alpentire Saints had visited Germany and seen these dogs previously. She had been planning to bring King into the country herself, but after she showed Ken Gaunt a photograph of King, he bought the dog and two bitches. One bitch died in whelp in quarantine, and the other never reproduced. Unfortunately, King was never used much at stud, and when Ken died he went to Marjorie Hindes and then subsequently to Reg James of the Gerunda kennels. The best of King's descendants in England came through Catherine. The other of the original two Swindridge sisters, Acacia, was mated to Ch. Burtonswood Bossy Boots and produced Ch. Swindridge Sir Dorian and Ch. Swindridge Madam Danielle, both smooth-coated. Dorian was then mated to Catherine, and the resulting son, Ch. Swindridge Ferdinand, was put to his half-sister Ch. Swindridge Geraldine (ex Catherine). From this liaison came Ch. Swindridge Mathew and Ch. Swindridge Madalene. In five years the Swindridge kennel produced five smooth Champions – not an easy feat, as smooths have always had to compete against the more popular rough-coated variety in Britain – and Michael and Ann's Swindridge kennel won the top breeders in 1983 and 1984. Ferdinand is the maternal grandfather of the present top-winning smooth, Ch. Winterbergs Boy. Ch. Swindridge Laura, one of the foundation bitches of the Schnozzer kennel of Mr and Mrs Girling, was bred the same way as Mathew and Madalene. Two others from this litter, Swindridge Luke and Lucinda, both won CCs, but unfortunately they died young. Madalene was out-crossed to our imported Ch. Pankraz von den drei Helmen of Bernmont, and one of the resulting dogs was Ch. Swindridge Rochester. Madalene was later put to Ch. Bernmont Murdoch to produce the lovely 'C' litter (the second time around). Two of these smooths, Swindridge Columbus and Swindridge Cassius, are currently winning in the show ring, and puppies sired by Columbus are showing exceptional promise. The latest Swindridge Champion is Ch. Swindridge Andrea, also a daughter of Murdoch. Michael has also pioneered the friendship between the English St Bernard breeders and those involved with the breed on the continent. He organised the first trip to the Amsterdam show in 1977. Return trips have been organised between the Dutch and the English St Bernard Club.

The Swindridge's first Champion was Ch. Benem Lady Guinevere, one of a litter of ten bred in Lincolnshire by Ron and Millie Miller – not to be confused with Ernie Millar of the Dail na Mine prefix. They were sired by Lucky Strike of Cornagarth out of My Lady Emma. Another member of this litter was Benem Lady Constance of Bernmont, the dam of Ch. Bernmont Nola. Nola was mated to the last male Cornagarth Champion, Cornagarth Dominant Dominic of Bernmont, and she produced Bernmont Diplomat, the father of Murdoch. Dominic was also the sire of the Bernmont 'A' litter which included Ch. Bernmont Aristocrat, Ch. Bernmont

Michael Wensley with Ch. Benem Lady Guinevere.

Alexandra and Astrid, winner of two CCs and owned by A. Otway. Mrs Joy Evans acquired Benem Sir Galahad as a rescue dog, and she campaigned him to win his title and to win Reserve in Working Group at Blackpool when he was six years old. He was the sire of her bitch, Ch. Morning Star of Hartleapwell, who when mated to Ch. Maurbry Message produced Ch. Hartleapwell Magic Moments and Ch. Hartleapwell Secret Love. Secret Love's progeny by Ch. Whaplode My Lord included Ch. Hartleapwell Midnite Magic, Ch. Hartleapwell Touch of Magic and Ch. Hartleapwell Stormy Magic, owned by Mr Barry Allen. These Hartleapwells

Ann Wensley with Ch. Swindridge Madalene and Ch. Swindridge Mathew.
won many CCs at the end of the eighties.

Ch. Maurbry Message was bred by Mrs Mary Chapman out of Ch. Whaplode Unique and Benem Lady Be Good, another member of the Benem litter. Mrs Chapman also bred Ch. Maurbry Modelman out of the same bitch and sired by Ch. Topvalley Wogans Winner. Mrs Chapman bought her first bitch in wartime, but, apart from owning Ch. Cornagarth Minty of Maurbry, her greatest successes came late in her life with these two dogs. She bred Ch. Maurbry Maisy Maiden, owned by Tim and Mandy Barnes. They bred the 1987 top dog, Ch. Coppice Bertie, using Maisy Maiden and Ch. Marlendar Moonraker. The latter was bred by Linda Martin, who has kept St Bernards in Wiltshire for several years, and is the present secretary of the South of England St Bernard Club. She recently won a CC with her eleven-month-old bitch Saranbeck Sayra, who is by Swindridge Columbus out of Ch. Saranbeck Sweep. The Saranbecks are bred by Diane Fawcett from Yorkshire, who has been in the breed for several years.

There are a number of St Bernard breeders of long standing, who, by coincidence, all live in Lincolnshire. Pauline and Brian Stammers of Ravensbank have had consistently good stock, and they bred and owned Ch. Ravensbank Hardtime and Ravensbank Simply Soloman of Sileeda, who was the sire of one of the present top winners, Ch. Lynbern Dennis The Menace of Meadowmead. Terry and Keith Ridings have also had quality stock in their Bavush kennels, including Ch. Bavush Drina. John, May and Helen Bateman started their Fastacre kennels in Wakefield in the mid-seventies, and then moved to Lincolnshire. They made up Ch. Knockespoch Highline of Fastacre, bred by Sue Roberts, and imported Int. Swedish and Norwegian Ch. Bernegardens J.R. from Sweden, which they also made an English Champion. They imported a bitch from the same kennel, Int. Ch. Berngardens Windsong. Mr Bateman instigated the start of the Eastern St Bernard Club in 1983 and was its first secretary, but resigned from this position early in the club's history. The present secretary is Mr Mick Thorpe, whose wife Kathy owns the Ljubavni Saints. She campaigned Footloose Freddy to win his title. The Arambaskh kennel, owned by Brian Markham, also started up in the eighties. He owned Ch. Woodruff Felicity and bred the well-known Arambaskh Statesman. The most recent kennel to move up to Lincolnshire is the Bernadinos, owned by Jill and Werner Lux. They made up three Champions from one litter: Ch. Bernadino Maxi, Ch. Bernadino Winterberg and Ch. Bernadino Fedor. They were sired by Ch. Topvalley Wogans Winner out of Ravensbank Katy Cube of Bernadino. They currently own Ch. Winterbergs Boy, top winner in 1990, who was bred by Richard Young out of Zermatt Contessa.

Trevor and Norma Goodwin have also bought two bitches from the Bernegarden kennels in Sweden, and recently they acquired a beautiful smooth dog, Norwegian Ch. Bernegardens Buckpasser. He has already gained his English title and we are likely to hear a lot more of him in the future. Paul and Jos Girling are another successful kennel to start in the eighties. They bred their best dog in their first litter, Ch. Schnozzer Huggy Bear, sired by Ch. Topvalley Wogans Winner. They have currently two home-bred Champions: Ch. Schnozzer Latest Edition and Ch. Schnozzer Dark Golden, who are by Huggy Bear out of their bitch, Ch. Swindridge Laura. The latest breeders to make their mark on the St Bernard scene are Bob and Lesley Byles. Their Ch. Lynbern Dennis The Menace of Meadowmead won many CCs in 1990, and they also made up two more Champions – Ch. Meadowmead Juliana, sired by English and Irish Champion Montaryie Galestorm out of Coatham Mary Rose, and Ch. Mountside Mauritania of Meadowmead, sired by Ravensbank Simply Soloman of Sileeda out of Coatham Britania.

Mauritania was bred in the north of England in the small but top-class Mountside

Jill Lux with Ch. Winterbergs Boy.

Ch. Lynbern Dennis The Menace of Meadowmead.

Owned by Mr and Mrs R. Byles.

Hartley.

*Eng. and
Nor. Ch.
Bernegardens
Buckpasser.
Owned by
Mrs Norma
Goodwin.*

*Michael M.
Trafford.*

*Hazel Churchill with Ch. Finetime Sputnik and Pat Churchill with Ch. Finetime The
Great Bear.* *Waring.*

kennel of Ray and Elaine Stokell. Their home-bred Ch. Mountside Movie Star won her title in 1990. She is from a litter by Ch. Finetime The Great Bear and Coatham Britania. Ch. Finetime The Great Bear was owned by Pat and Hazel Churchill at their Finetime kennels. He was bred by Hazel and her previous partner, Geoffrey Findlay, from Arambaskh Statesman and Pilgrimwood Gorgeous Girl. His litter sister, Finetime Sputnik, is also a Champion. The first Finetime Champion was Finetime Sardonyx. His litter sister was Ch. Finetime Amethyst of Bernmont, who won Best of Breed at Crufts in 1987. Her owner is Mrs Iris Sobolewski, who was a complete newcomer to the breed at the time. She opened her winning account with her first prize, her first CC, and Best of Breed at Crufts – in one day! The Bear sired three Champions in one litter – Ch. Finetime Celtic Princess, Ch. Finetime Saxon Alchemist and Ch. Finetime Temptress, owned by Mr and Mrs Bradley. He is also the sire of Val and John Taylor's home-bred Champion, Ch. Earl of Alvaston, and Ch. My Lucky Lady.

There have been very few breeders in Scotland since the days of the Misses Pratt with their Berndean kennel. Miss R. M. Bryce had considerable success in the early fifties. She bred an exceptional litter of four Champions from Ch. Yew Tree St Christopher and Beldene Josephine. She kept Ch. Mairead Masterpiece and Ch. Mairead Indian Prince herself; Ken Gaunt won with Ch. Cornagarth Culzean Nero – this dog was the model for the silver St Bernard trophy given by Hennessey Cognac for Best of Breed at Crufts; and Mrs Whiteley made up Ch. Cornagarth McNab. The latter was no doubt owned at one time by Ken Gaunt. In earlier times it was quite permissible for anyone to register a dog that they owned with their own prefix on the front or back of the name. Today, if the dog is not bred by the owner, the prefix must follow the name, and if bred by the owner, it precedes the name. Miss Bryce also bred Mairead Angus McNab from Masterpiece out of her own Ch. Snowbound Cynthea.

Mrs Judy McMurray started in the breed in the sixties, and she imported two Saints from the Klara Kloster kennels in the seventies, just after Cornagarth had bought King. She had the honour of winning the Working Group at Crufts in 1976 with Ch. Snowranger Cascade, bred by Clare Bradley and Peter Hill. This dog was used as the model for a brooch and other jewellery sold by the St Bernard Club of Scotland. Mrs McMurray's beautiful home-bred bitch, Ch. Alpentire Paters Princess, sired by Ch. Cornagarth Burtonswood Be Great out of Snowranger Fforrest Charm won many CCs. Miss Jean Fyffe bred many St Bernards in Carnoustie at around the same time. Her Claypottis Lady Aurora was mated to Ch. Christcon St Jeremy, and this produced her only Champion, Ch. Panbride Lady Freda. Aurora was quite a character, and she used to take herself for a walk of several miles, and then catch

Bavush Stormin Normam: A top winning puppy in 1991. Owned by Keith and Terry Ridings.

Ch. Laird o' Glaya of Treeburn. Owned by Bob and Olive Gardner. Hartley.

the bus home. She waited at the bus stop where it picked her up, and she was put off at the stop for home. We often wondered if Miss Fyffe was given the bill for these unaccompanied trips!

The smooth-coated Ch. Panbride Sir Warren of Pittforth was owned by Matt and Celia Whitelaw. Their Pittforth kennels have been the most successful Scottish kennel since the war. They bought a bitch, Ch. Cornagarth Heike of Pittforth, from the Gaunts and they showed her and made her a Champion. They won Best of Breed at Crufts in 1975 with their home-bred Ch. Pittforth Angus, a son of Heike and Ch. Cornagarth Burtonswood Be Great. Heike's second litter to Sir Warren gave them Ch. Pittforth Calum, a dog of immense proportions, Ch. Pittforth Catriona, and the smooth Pittforth Cassandra. Ch. Catriona was the dam of their last Champion, Pittforth Fleur, who died recently at eleven years of age. Her sire was Whaplode Julian of Bernmont. We had Ch. Irrissa of Bernmont from the same litter. The Whitelaws also won two CCs with Pittforth Gillian, out of the same sire and Cassandra. Bob and Olive Gardner of the Treeburn St Bernards had Smokey Bear of Treeburn, also a CC winner, from the same litter as Gillian. Bear, a smooth, was the sire of their home-bred smooth Champion, Ch. Treeburn Boulevard Beauty. They won Best of Breed at the St Bernard Club of Scotland Championship Show in 1984 with Ch. Laird o' Glayva of Treeburn.

Times have changed from the days when the Cornagarth kennels ruled the ring, and it is unlikely that we will ever see their like again. Seventy-five Champions bore the Cornagarth prefix in England, while the highly successful Burtonswood kennel produced twenty-five Champions. Marjorie Hindes always worked very closely with Ken and Kathleen Gaunt, and their Cornagarth/Burtonswood stock is in most English-bred stock today. The Cornagarth prefix came to an end when Mrs Gaunt died suddenly in 1974, followed a year later by her husband, who was shattered by her death. He had been in poor health for many years following a coronary and never expected his wife to pre-decease him. Miss Hindes still shows in a small way. The Peldartor and Bernmont kennels have both produced fifteen Champions, and Lindenhall, Swindridge and Coatham have now reached double figures in their tally of Champions.

Chapter Seven

THE ST BERNARD IN NORTH AMERICA

The first St Bernard to have any impact in America was Plinlimmon. He was brought to the U.S.A. from England by an American actor, Mr Emmet, who showed him in theatres in several American cities. He was very large and many people were so inspired by his magnificent appearance that they wanted to own a St Bernard. Plinlimmon was bred by F. Smith from Ch. Pilgrim out of Bessie II. The other early imports were Lord Bute, bought for 4,000 dollars, Sir Bedivere purchased for 7,000 dollars, and Madam Bedivere, purchased for 3,000 dollars. Both Bute and Madam Bedivere were owned by Knowles Croskey of Philadelphia. The best St Bernard at Westminster in 1886 was Merchant Prince, who was by Bayard out of Pastime. He was owned by E. H. Moore of Melrose, Massachussets. He had won twenty cups and prizes in England prior to his export to America, and he went on to sire many winners in his new home. However, one of the first St Bernards to be registered with the National American Kennel Club was Chief, born in May 1879 and owned by Mr Goicowria of New York and bred by Mr J. P. Haines of Toms River, New Jersey. He was by Harold out of Judy. Miss Anna H. Whitney had Saints registered in the early breed stud book: a long-haired dog called Hermit, a long-haired bitch called Nun, and three short-haired bitches, Alma, Brunhilde and Chartreuse. The stud books were later taken over by the American Kennel Club. There were several 'Hectors' registered in this era. Ch. Hector, born 20.2.1894, A.K.C. 4425, bred by Henry

Schumacher and imported by Mr E. E. Hopf of the Hospice Kennels of Arlington, New Jersey, can be found in many of the early pedigrees.

The St Bernard Club of America was founded in 1888 by a group of the prominent fanciers of the time, many of whom had imported dogs from England. Although most of their stock was imported from England, the club decided to be governed by the International Breed Standard that had been formed in Zurich in 1887. This immediately caused consternation as all the owners of English-bred St Bernards judged them according to the English Standard. St Bernards were very popular in America at this time, just as they were in Europe, and dogs were imported for millions of dollars. The 1890 New York show had one hundred and fifty-one St Bernards competing, the Chicago show had fifty-eight entries, and the Boston Show had fifty-nine entries. At all other shows the St Bernard entry was double that of the previous year.

The president of the newly-formed St Bernard Club was Mr W. H. Joeckel Jnr. of Bloomfield, New Jersey; Miss Anna H. Whitney of Lancaster, Massachussets was one of the vice presidents, and Mr J. C. Thurston, New York, was the secretary. The St Bernard Club of America was revamped in 1897 when ten men formed a new club, with no reference to the previous one. It was formed in Grand Rapids, Michigan. Mr Dudley E. Waters was secretary/treasurer and Col. Jacob Ruppert Jnr was president. The club started with fifty-eight members. Mr Waters remained in office until his death in 1931 when Mr M. T. Vanden Bosch of Grand Rapids took over and helped to reorganise the St Bernard Club of America for the second time. In March 1932 Mr Joseph Mulray of Newtown Square, Pennsylvania and Mr Leroy E. Fess of Williamsville, New York ran the club's affairs until a meeting on February 13th 1933, held at the Hotel Victoria, New York City, when officers and governors of the club were elected. During the last thirty years the St Bernard Club of America had been fairly inactive, and the breed in America had degenerated. This was mainly because there had been no attempt to improve the quality of the dogs. Many of the puppies had been bred by dog dealers rather than specialist breeders with a love of the breed. The typical American St Bernard was still mainly influenced by the English type, despite the acceptance of the International Standard nearly fifty years before.

Joseph H. Fleischli of Springfield, Illinois was elected as president of the newly-formed club, and vice presidents were Paul R. Forbriger, William Gartner and Paul G. Tilenius, all from Brooklyn, New York. The secretary/treasurer was Mrs Eleanor J. Dalton of Stamford, Connecticut and the governors were Eleanor Cavanagh, Eleanor J. Dalton, Joseph H. Fleischli, Paul R. Forbriger, Alice H. French, William Gartner, Arthur Hesser, Joseph T. Mulray, Robert Nicholson, Jessyn S. Robinson,

Paul G. Tilenius, Leo C. Urlaub, Gottlieb Zulliger and Agnes Kemp, whose descendants are still breeding St Bernards today under her Carmen prefix.

Joseph Fleischli drew up a proclamation which was accepted by most of the club members. It read:

"Among the breeders, fanciers and judges of the St Bernard breed in America there seems to be an obscurity how the correct type, which was established in the International Standard and accepted by the St Bernard Club of America at its founding in the year 1888, is to be conceived. The difference between the International Standard and the English Standard is visibly very small. Therefore this cannot be the reason for the various head types, which are known here as the English type, contrary to those bred in Switzerland and Germany. Both of these countries, as well as America, have the International Standard and thus it is clear that one of the two types is right, while the other is wrong, as long as both types are judged according to the viewpoints of the International Standard, unless the International Standard can be freely interpreted according to the opinion of the judges in various countries.

"Therefore, the resolution was established, that the St Bernard Club of America acknowledge that interpretation of the International Standard as correct and official, which interpretation is acknowledged by the Swiss and the German clubs. Both clubs, as well as the American, judge according to the International Standard.

"It is further resolved that the St Bernard Club of America condemns all other interpretations of the Standard as incorrect. This applies especially to England, who did not accept the International Standard but followed its own standard.

"It is furthermore resolved that the St Bernard Club of America kindly requests all judges of the American Kennel Club to judge the St Bernard Dog according to the International Standard, particularly in the manner in which it is interpreted in Switzerland, the home of the St Bernard, and in Germany, and accepted by the St Bernard Club of America, so that the right and correct type will be secured in America, the same as in Central Europe."

Mr Joseph Fleischli was the son of Franz Fleischli born in Lucerne, Switzerland. Mr Franz Fleischli founded the Edelweiss kennels in 1894, and his son started breeding St Bernards from 1908. It was Mr Joseph Fleischli who imported many good dogs from Switzerland and Germany. Other main importers of the time were Gottlieb Zulliger, a native of Switzerland, living in Barron, Wisconsin, Leo C. Urlaub, and a few others who were mainly officers of the club. Mr Fleischli acquired the great Ch. Kavalier vom Grossglockner from an American car manufacturer, who had imported the dog from Germany. But perhaps his most famous import was Ch. Gerd v d Lueg v Edelweiss, winner of twenty-one Best in Shows, forty-six Best Working Groups, over a hundred Best of Breeds, and the St Bernard Club of America National Specialty three times, in 1950, 1951 and 1952. He was Best of Sex in 1948, beaten for Best of Breed by his sister, Ch. Gerda v d Lueg of Alpine Plateau. Gerda won the Best Opposite Sex in 1951. They were bred by Ernest Grossenbacher from a mating by Elmar v d Lueg and Bella v Ringelli. In 1949 Best of Breed at the National Specialty was won by another of Mr Fleischli's imports, Ch. Gero Oenz v Edelweiss. He had been bred by E. Wuthrich out of Sieger Emir von Melina and Siegerin Erga Oenz. Gero Oenz went on to win five Best in Shows. Fleischli had previously won Best of Breed at the National Specialty with another of his imports, Ch. Esbo v Grossglockner. Some of Fleischli's other imports were Ch. Nanni Deppler, Helma Oenz v Edelweiss and Bella v Menzberg. Ch. Joggi Oenz v Edelweiss, brother of Gero Oenz from a later litter, was owned by Odessa Llewellyn of Waukee, Iowa.

Back in the thirties a large amount of stock was imported from the bloodlines of Int. Ch. Emir vom Jura. Paul R. Forbiger of Brooklyn bought Int. Ch. Rasko v d Reppisch in 1933, and this dog completed his American Championship in one and a half weeks. At the first recorded St Bernard Club of America National Specialty Show, on May 25th 1935, Rasko won Best of Breed, despite being seven and a half years old. The following year Rasko was exhibited 'Not For Competition' when Mr Fleischli was the judge. Best of Breed was Irwin Cohn's import, Ch. Rigo von Rigi. A daughter of Rasko was awarded Winners Bitch. Along with Rasko, Mr Forbiger imported Dora Belmont, Berna v d Lueg, Athos von Hochfield and three others from England: St Scholastica Pearl, St John Pearl and Lady Veronica – some of the top English Saints at the time. Mr Forbiger also owned Ch. Hercuveens Invincible, a well-known dog of the time. The Hercuveens kennel was one of the most famous dogs in the States during the twenties and thirties, but they were of the old American or English type, which Mr Fleischli had condemned in his club resolution. However, this did not stop Ch. Hercuveen Standard, owned by the Vindoba kennels of Staten Island, New York, from winning Best of Breed at the 1938 National. The continentals triumphed again the following year when Ch. Junie des Tourelles won the 1938 Specialty. She was a daughter of Rasko and his fellow import Dora Belmont.

Among the other imports in the thirties were the long-haired dogs from Switzerland: Barry v Oschwand, Pluto v Altachen, Nero v Multenrain, Tell v Lotten, Cid von Eiger and Sieger Apollo v Rougang. The short-haired imports included: Lola v Rigi, Palace v Rigi, Sieger Vallo v Rigi and the German imports Tasso v

Goppingen, Odschi von Margothof, Varus v Grossglockner, Porthos v Falkenstein, Doldi v Grossglockner and Armin v d Teck; all the German dogs were long-haired with the exception of Armin. The first St Bernard kennel to be registered with the American Kennel Club was the Carmen kennels owned by Mr T. E. L. Kemp, in 1903. He imported St Bernards from Holland, Switzerland and Germany and had started showing in 1899 and one of their better known dogs was Ch. Queen Flora II. Mrs Agnes Kemp was one of the first women all-round judges in the U.S.A. and Canada, and their daughter Mrs Rita Holmes was one of the six founder members of the New England St Bernard Club, with her husband Harold twice elected as president. Their daughter Janice Myers continued the family tradition and is also actively involved in the Carmen kennels.

The Second World War did not have such a drastic effect on the St Bernard in America as it did in Europe, although there were no National Specialties held in 1944 or 1945. The 1946 National Specialty Show was won by Ch. Apollo of Alpine Plateau, owned by his breeder A. F. Hayes. Apollo was a grandson of Rasko v d Reppisch and Esbo v Grossglockner. The Alpine Plateau kennels was one of the most successful of the time. Besides his Gerda v d Lueg, they also imported Barri v Huttwil and Falco Oenz. Other Alpine Plateau Champions included Ch. Questor of Alpine Plateau and Ch. Maida of Alpine Plateau. Mr Hayes bred the Best of Breed at the 1943 National Specialty Show with Ch. Mountain Ranger owned by Mr and Mrs Jarvis of San Francisco. This dog was by Rasrakko v Ticino – a son of Rasko – out of Queen of the Alps. Mr and Mrs Jarvis imported Ch. Horsa v Zwing Uri just after World War II.

Some of the other post-war imports were Mira vom Rigi imported by Don Diesner, and the brother and sister Ch. Falco vom Rigi and Siegerin Fortuna vom Rigi, imported by Mr and Mrs Parker of the Sunny Slopes kennels. Mr Stanley Bussinger owned the short-haired imports Minka v Immenburg and Ch. Major v Neu Habsburg, and Mr Victor Bitterman imported the German bitch Katja v Ludwigstein. Mr Herbert Heilman owned Ch. Aline v d Roth, a short-haired daughter of Gerd v d Lueg. Aline's litter brother Also v d Roth was imported by Mr John Friend of Hartland, Wisconsin. Mr Hayes had several Champions under his Heilmans kennel name. Ch. Heilmans Eris v Gero won Best of Breed at the 1955 National, Ch. Heilmans Julia v Gerd was Best Opposite Sex at the 1953 National, and Ch. Heilmans Katy v Gero was Best in Show at the 1957 National.

Mr Lawrence Powell was another great breeder of the post-war years. His first great dog was believed to be Ch. King Laddie Rasko Whitebread, born in June 1941 and bred by Norma F. Keller. He was by Prince Rasko of Tall Maples, a son of Rasko v d Reppisch, and Bretwalda of Tall Maples, a granddaughter of Rasko v d

Reppisch, and his wins included Best of Breed at the Westminster Show in 1946, Best of Breed at the New York Specialty Show, and Dog Of The Year All Breeds. Other Powell Champions followed, including Ch. Powells Little John, Ch. Powells Tristan of Riga, Ch. Powells Lady Lee, Ch. Powells Laurette Lee and Ch. Powells Dawn O'Day.

Mrs Beatrice Knight started her world-famous Sanctuary Woods kennels mainly based on Alpine Plateau stock, plus the imported Ch. Banz von Bachingerhof, who went to her on the recommendation of Arthur Hesser. Banz had already been imported by a New Yorker in 1951. The Sanctuary Woods kennels has bred over a hundred Champions: the most well-known were Ch. Sanctuary Woods Fantabulous, Ch. Sanctuary Woods Going My Way and Ch. Sanctuary Woods Gulliver. Ch. Sanctuary Woods Better Times won Best of Breed at the National Specialty Show in 1960. Other Sanctuary Woods Saints to take this honour were Ch. Sanctuary Woods Four Winds in 1964, Ch. Sanctuary Woods Going My Way in 1970, Ch. Sanctuary Woods Justice in 1971 and Ch. Sanctuary Woods Litany in 1975. Ch. Sanctuary Woods Reverie won Best of Sex at the 1956 National, Ch. Sanctuary Woods Nita Nannette won the same award in 1963, Ch. Sanctuary Woods Kleona was Best in Show for three years in succession, 1971, 1972 and 1973, and Ch. Sanctuary Woods Litany was Best of Sex in 1974. Mrs Knight is now well into her eighties and the Sanctuary Woods kennel is still in operation. Mrs Knight judged the sweepstakes at the 1988 Centennial Show nearly fifty years after obtaining her first St Bernard as a pet. She first fell in love with the breed when she was seven years old, when she saw a picture of a St Bernard. She did not see another representative of the breed until she went to a dog show in San Diego in 1935 where there was only one St Bernard being exhibited. Mrs Knight had been asked to present the trophies, but this meeting with Silver Side King, who came from Eastern Washington, changed her life and she has kept the show catalogue to this day as a souvenir. She bought her first St Bernard in 1939 for ten dollars; the bitch had only three good legs as she had been kicked by a horse. Mrs Knight did not know anything about dogs then, but she loved her first St Bernard dearly. She first applied for the Sanctuary Woods prefix in 1948 and her success in the breed has been unrivalled. She says that when she hears a dog's name she can still see it in living colour. This remarkable lady with half a century's experience behind her, still likes to encourage the novice Saint lover, remembering that she was once a novice herself. The Saint Bernard Club of America's Catalogue for its centenary show had the following inscription on the first page: The St Bernard Club of America proudly dedicates this centennial celebration to Mrs Beatrice Knight of Sanctuary Woods Kennels for her contribution and dedication to the St Bernard Dog." The Subira kennel, now owned by William and

Ch. Grieco's Endorsement von W.O.A. with his sons Ch. Star's Chaparrel v Boris and Ch. Subira's The General v Boris.

Judith Buell and Sandra Rodrigo was started in the fifties by Lillian Buell. Her Ch. Nelda of Birchwood produced twenty-seven Champions, including Ch. Subira's Casper The Viking, who won one hundred and twenty-seven Best of Breeds. The sire of Casper, and of most of the Subira Champions was Ch. Subira's Crackerjack out of Ch. Subira's Crackerjody. Casper won Best of Breed at the National Specialty in Santa Barbara in 1967 and was the top winning St Bernard in 1968 and 1969. He was owned by Eleanor Keaton, wife of the comedian Buster Keaton. The dog was handled by William Buell, who is a top professional handler. There have been innumerable other Subira Champions over the years. Ch. Subira's Claim To Fame is currently one of the leading dogs in America. He is owned by Howard Dees and Megan Buell. Megan, who is William and Judith's daughter, is one of the top junior handlers in America.

Arthur Hesser first owned St Bernards in 1919, and he was one of the people involved in the reorganised club in 1932. He judged the National Specialty on many occasions. He had a wide knowledge of the St Bernards in Switzerland and Germany, and he advised many people on their imports. Herman A. Peabody was another well-known breeder of the fifties and sixties. He owned several Champions under his Brownhelms prefix, including Ch. Sweet Sue of Brownhelm, Ch. Mr Jody of Brownhelm and Ch. Hildas Helga of Brownhelm.

Ch. Subira's Claim To Fame.   *Bergman.*

The vom Rigi, Oenz, Grossglockner, v d Lueg, v Zwing Uri, and v Melina kennels had been the chief source of the American imports in the thirties and forties, but by the late fifties and sixties most of these great names were gone, and American breeders turned to the Sauliamt kennels of Edward Rodel for the majority of their Swiss imports. These included Ch. Lord v Sauliamt, winner of the National in 1959, Am. & Can. Ch. Xano v Sauliamt, Ch. Figaro v Sauliamt, Ch. Zetto v Sauliamt, Ch. Gerlo v Sauliamt, winner Best of Reserve at the National in 1968 and Ch. Cambo v Sauliamt. In 1959 Mrs Winnifred Martin imported Basko v Salmegg, who was sired by Sieger Roy von Neu Habsburg. Basko gained his American Championship and produced some excellent stock. Mrs Martin owns the Prairieaire kennels, which is still active in the breed and has had many successes with dogs such as Ch. Prairieaire Rox v Zwing Basko, a son of Basko, who won the stud dog class at the National Specialty in 1966, and more recently with Ch. Prairieaire's Ghost of Rox, Ch. Prairieaire's Long John, Ch. Prairieaire's Bullion, Ch. Prairieaire's Quincy and Ch. Prairieaire's Stormtrooper.

The Shagg Bark kennels of William and Elizabeth Roberts was a well-known kennel of the sixties. They owned and bred Ch. Bowser Waller, winner of a hundred

Ch. Opdyke's Fair Warning, handled by Giovanni Morsiani.

Best of Breeds, twenty-eight Group firsts, and five Best in Shows. He was a grandson of Ch. Faust von Melina. One of Bowser's best-known sons was Ch. Shagg Barks Buddy. Rex Roberts owned Wunderbar von Narbenholt and Ch. Hagen von Narben, and they won Best Brace in Show at Westminster in 1963. Grace Harvey of the Zwinghof kennels was active in the breed during this period. Her Ch. Harvey's Zwingo Barri v Banz won four Best in Shows and ten Group firsts. He won Best of Breed at the 1961 National Specialty. Zwingo was the sire of many winners, and Zwinghof Champions included Ch. Zwinghof Jeanne, Ch. Zwinghof Jumbo, Ch. Zwinghof Xeobo and Ch. Zwinghof Wonna Joggi.

Marlene and Douglas Anderson started breeding St Bernards in 1961 and established their Beau Cheval kennels. They started the kennels as a hobby on the advice of Marlene's doctor, as she suffered from Multiple Sclerosis and he recommended that she took up an occupation to give her something to think about. Then they went to a show, and her husband, handling a dog in the show ring for the first time, won a four point major. The Beau Cheval kennels in Bucks County, Pennsylvania developed from there and they housed between fifty and seventy-five St Bernards at any one time. There were an impressive number of Beau Cheval Champions including Ch. Beau Cheval's Shamrock Mardoug, Ch. Beau Cheval's Tralee Mardoug, Ch. Beau Cheval's Tablo Mardoug, Ch. Beau Cheval's Padre Mardoug, Ch. Beau Cheval's Helsinki Mardoug, Ch. Beau Cheval's Della Mardoug, Ch. Beau Cheval's Golden Cesar and Am. & Can. Ch. Beau Cheval's Mt Lesa Mardoug.

Serendipity is the kennel name of Judith Goldman, and she owned many Champions including Am. & Can. Ch. Serendipity's Tertius, born in 1964. Ch. Serendipity's Pussycat and Ch. Serendipity's Molly Brown were both from Ch. Serendipity's Octavius out of Ch. Serendipity's Secunda – but from different litters. Molly Brown was owned by Richard and Nancy Steinberger of the Opdyke kennels. There was no National Specialty held in 1962, but the following year Ch. Switzer of Shady Hollow was the winner and Best Opposite Sex went to Ch. Gerda Christina of Skycroft. She won twenty-three Best of Breeds and five Group placings, but her wins were overshadowed by her litter brother Ch. Gero Christopher of Skycroft, who won six Best in Shows, twenty-two Group firsts and eighty-two Best of Breeds. Ch. Skycroft's Hercules won Best of Breed at the 1965 National in Illinois. The Skycroft kennels were owned by Shirlie Cox and Marjorie Steele and among their Champions were: Ch. Skycroft Lancelot, Ch. Skycroft Lady Crystal and Ch. Skycroft Lucinda of Opdyke. Lucinda was owned by Diane Radcliffe, who owns the Opdyke kennels with her husband, Glenn, and this is one of the most successsful kennels in America today. Glenn Radcliffe and Richard Steinberger owned Ch. Saturno del Soccorso, who came from Dr Morsiani's kennels in Italy. Saturno was the sire of Am. & Can. Ch. Opdyke's Hair, bred by Richard Steinberger and owned by Marcia Carter. Hair was a Champion by the time he was seventeen and a half months old, and he went on to win three Best in Show All Breeds and forty Group firsts. He was the top winning St Bernard in 1977. Int. Ch. Am. Mex. Ch. Mar-dons Buckpasser v Opdyke was another successful son of Saturno. He won one hundred and twenty-five Best of Breeds, twelve Best in Shows All Breeds, including two in Mexico. Buckpasser was bred by Richard and Nancy Steinberger and owned by Marcia Carter and Don Breazeale. Ch. Opdyke's Pure Sugar was Best Opposite Sex at the National in 1976 and 1977. She was owned by Glenn Radcliffe and Richard Steinberger, co-owner of the Opdyke kennel. Ch. Stanridge's Thor of Opdyke, bred by John Stanek was another fine representative of the Opdyke kennels. John Stanek owned the Stanridge kennels with Benjamin Ridgeway of Columbus, New Jersey, and their dogs were based on Powells and Riga stock.

One of the most famous American St Bernards of the time was Ch. Titan v Mallen. He was bred by Lou Mallen from Ch. Lance's Robin Hood out of Phoebe v Mallen. He won the National Specialty twice in 1969 and 1972. His sire, Ch. Lance's Robin Hood, was the father of many top winning dogs in the country at the time. He was bred by B. Henry and owned by the Saint Retreat kennel of Dr George Wessar. Some of his best progeny include Ch. Saint Retreat's Robin Hood, Ch. Saint Retreat's Peanuts, Ch. Saint Retreat's Batman II, Ch. Saint Retreat's Image and Ch. Templehof's Zeus v Lance. Zeus was the first home-bred Champion of Terry and Sara Temple, well-known for their Forever Saints. Terry was a judge at the 1988 Centennial Show. He had his first St Bernard in 1964 and made up his first Champion in 1966. Their successes continued through the years, and Ch. Forever Moxie won Best Opposite Sex at the 1987 National. Moxie's litter-mate is Ch. Forever Gotcha, and the Temples also own Moxie and Gotcha's dam, Ch. High Chateau Forever Bliss. Another of the Centennial judges was Mr Gerald E. Wallin. He and his wife, Gloria, owned Ch. The Khan, a son of Ch. Titan v Mallen and Liesl von Mallen. The Khan was always handled by his co-owner Gerald Wallin, who owned him in partnership with his breeder David Forrest, and he was the top owner-handled St Bernard in 1972 and 1973 and won over fifty Best of Breeds.

Don and Marcia Carter started breeding St Bernards in the sixties using their Mar-Don prefix, and today they are both American Kennel Club licensed judges of St Bernards. The Carters' Am. & Can. Ch. Opdyke's Hair was joint top stud dog in 1978; he was the sire of Ch. Mar-Don's Joshua v Unity, Ch. Mar-Don's King Cotton Bear, who won Best Puppy at the National Specialty in 1977, and Ch. Vindale's Bit Of Money. The Carters also owned Ch. Kutus Little Boy Brandy, the overall top stud dog in 1979. He was the sire of Ch. Mar-Don's Ben Franklin, Ch. Mar-Don's Patrick Henry and Ch. Vol's All Alone v Mar-Don, Ch. Vol's Banjo Girl v Mar-Don and Ch. Vol's Buffy v Bud. These last three Champions also secured the joint top brood bitch title for their mother, Ch. Mar-Don's Missy Moe Bud, owned by Dingus and Carter.

Vic Dingus of the Vol Kennels owned Ch. Love Saints Mister Oscar, who was bred by Spencer and Alana Traub, and previously owned by Vic Dingus in partnership with Marcia Carter. Mister Oscar was among the top ten St Bernards in 1978 and 1979; he was by Ch. Kutu's Little Boy Brandy and Ch. Candy v Brandy L'ourse Alpine. Candy was one of the numerous Champions bearing the L'ourse Alpine prefix of Andre von Osch of Indiana. Ch. Little L'ourse Alpine, owned by Carol Worman, won Winners Bitch at the 1965 National Specialty. Ch. Apollo L'ourse Alpine, owned by Alan Crumbaker, was by Ch. Little Brutus L'ourse Alpine out of

Ch. Siegfried's Nero.   *Langdon.*

Windy L'ourse Alpine. Windy (the daughter of the famous Ch. Yogi L'ourse Alpine) was the mother of Xyleta L'ourse Alpine, born in 1965 and owned in the late sixties by Pat (Muggleton) and her mother in the U.K. She was sired by Coca Hill's Brutus and was an excellent sound bitch, with a very strong muzzle and head, with a good stop, but she was shorter than English bitches and she found little favour in the English show ring. Her highest award was third in the Open Bitch class at the Paignton Championship Show in 1969. However, many of her progeny lived to be twelve and thirteen years old, an age very seldom reached by English-bred St Bernards.

Mardonof was the prefix of Mary Lou and Donald Dube, and their famous import, Ch. Figaro v Sauliamt, was the sire of Can. Ch. Mardonof's Echo of Figaro. Ch.

*Ch. Ivo Madame
v Majoshof,
owned by
Michael Sherman*

Mardonof's Duplicate of Image was the son of Am. & Can. Ch. Mardonof's Image of Figaro and Ch. Mardonof's Duchess Melina. Possibly the most famous of the Mardonofs was the beautiful short-haired Ch. Hunk von Mardonof, owned by Col. W. Hagel, who used Siegfried as his kennel name (a prefix used by Albert de la Rie in Holland). Hunk was top stud dog for three years in succession: in 1975 he held the title jointly with Ch. Alpine Acre Baron v Shagg Bark, and then he took sole honours in 1976 and 1977. His Champion progeny in 1975 were Ch. Siegfried's Bella CDX, Ch. Siegfried's Hans Brinker (out of the Dutch import, Siegfried Mieke von Majoshof from Martin Zwerts) and Ch. Siegfried's Rita. In 1976 six of his progeny won their Championship titles: Ch. Baranof's Jenny Lind, Ch. Ladara's Hunsy von Hunk, Ch. Siegfried's Anjannette, Ch. Siegfried's Belinda, Ch. Sultan von Baranof and Ch. Truus von Baranof. A further six of his children won their Championships in 1977: these were Ch. Liesl von Baranof, Ch. Price's von Hunk, Ch. Saundalin's Giovanni, Ch. Siegfried's Astarte, Ch. Siegfried's Baby Harmony and Ch. Siegfried's Hunky Dori. Col. Hagel was the largest importer of Saints at this time, importing over twenty dogs, mainly from Holland and Switzerland as well as from Italy and Germany.

The Siegfried kennels are now in the ownership of Gus Stefanou and he is keeping

Ch. Vieledanke Ali D'Ranchett (Ch. Zappal's Vontare – Ranchett's High Hope).

MikRon Photos.

up the tradition of importing dogs from Europe. Ch. Ike Siegfried von Majoshof, born in 1984, came from the kennels of Martin Zwerts in Holland. He was a son of Int. Ch. Ashbjorn v d Enchial (Ashbjorn was also the father of Pat's imported Johan v h Wapen v Capelle of Bernmont) and Siegfried's Madame von Gleck. Ch. Xilla vom Norfbach, sired by Ch. Bobo v d Schillerwiessen out of Tanya v Norfbach, was imported from the German kennels of J. Titz. Ch. Ike Siegfried von Majoshof's brother is Ch. Ivo Madame v Majoshof, owned by Michael Sherman from Poway. Michael is well-known in continental Europe where he is a frequent visitor, and he sometimes exhibits his own dogs. Dogs may travel between America and Europe, with the exception of the U.K., Norway, Sweden and Finland, which have quarantine restrictions. Mr Sherman currently has two very nice imports from Denmark – Kongeaaen's Debbie, bred by Yrsa and Carl Otto Mastrup, born October 1988 and

Ch. Vieledanke Michael J (Ch. Maximum Vieledanke – Ch. Opdyke's Madonna).
Callea.

sired by Int. Ch. Sankt Cardi Anton out of Sherman's Santa Rose, and Hanaethorp Bea, also born in October 1988 and sired by Anton, but out of Hanaethorp Ruby. Bea was bred by Else and Arjen de Boer. When Pat judged the Californian Specialty show in 1990 she awarded this bitch first in the 12-18 months bitch class. A year later when Michael (Wensley) judged the show he awarded her the Winners Bitch.

Ch. Zappala's Vontare Vieledanke, born in May 1972, was owned by Carmelo and Cheryl Zappala and bred by Tom and Pearl Thank. This dog was an All Breeds Best in Show winner and a multiple Group winner. He was by Ch. Vieledanke Gombu, a son of Ch. Sanctuary Woods Gulliver and Des Neiges Eternelles Kati-Did. Kati-Did was also a top brood bitch. She was the dam of nine Champions including Ch. Zappala's Vontare Vieledanke and Ch. Vieledanke Ali D'Ranchett, who was the top St Bernard in the U.S.A. in 1982. Ch. Maximum Vieledanke and Ch. Vieledanke Michael J. also came from the Vieledanke kennels. The Zappalas are familiar figures at the European shows. Carmelo Zappala sometimes handles Int. Ch. Angie von Irmengrund for the Schonlebers when he is in Germany. They also own Ch. Folklore's Jubilee. Folklore is the prefix of Joanne Alstede, who is vice president of the St Bernard Club of America. Cheryl Zappala is one of the governors of the club.

In 1988 the St Bernard Club of America celebrated its centenary, and it is interesting to see which kennels and breeders played a significant part in the National Specialty in that historic year. The Opdyke kennels, which started breeding St Bernards in the sixties, completely dominated proceedings with Ch. Opdyke's Fair Warning, owned by Glenn Radcliffe, winning Best of Breed, and Best Opposite Sex and Best Winners bitch going to Opdyke's Emerald, owned by Glenn Radcliffe and Wayne Paup. The Reserve Winners Dog was Opdyke's Lancaster, owned by Glenn Radcliffe, Reserve Winners bitch was Opdyke's American Woman. The 12-18 month dog class winner was Opdyke's Tucumseh, owned by Glenn and Leslie Radcliffe, and Opdyke's Britton, also owned by Glenn and Leslie, won the class for American-bred bitches.

The remaining top award at the Centennial – Winners Dog – was won by Hezekiah von Rijn, owned by Bob and Sherry Sykora. The von Rijns is one of the present top winning kennels, and Ch. Ada von Rijn is one of their top winners. Bob Sykora is president of the St Bernard Club of America. The Open Long-haired dog class was won by Cache Retreat King Winter, owned by J. Lemieux and Ivan Palmblad. Mr Palmblad is the owner of the Cache Retreat kennels, and in partnership with R. White he won the 6-9 month puppy bitch class with Cache Retreat Glacier Melt. Other well-known Cache Retreat Saints include: Ch. Cache Retreat Zest For Life, Ch. Cache Retreat Taj Mahal, Ch. Cache Retreat Quintanne, Ch. Cache Retreat Partly Sunny, Ch. Cache Retreat Yearn for Fame, Ch. Cache Retreat M'Lord Banner and Ch. Cache Retreat Eclipse – these latter two were the parents of Glacier Melt.

The highly successful Stoans kennels, owned by Stan and Joan Zielinski, won Best Puppy at the Centennial with Stoan's Umelko of Jaz. He is the younger sister of Ch. Stoan's Kiska of Jaz, and they are both sired by Ch. Belyn's Journey v Exchequer out of Ch. Lynch Creek's A Zelda Stoan. Zelda was sired by Ch. Stoan's Nicholas of Klafa. High Chateau's Nestor was Best American Bred at this memorable show. He was owned by J. Fitzgerald and bred by P. Thiebault. He was sired by Ch. High

Chateau's Cesar out of Ch. Mt Olympus Desert Flower. High Chateau was Horst and Winifred Vogel's kennel name. Ch. High Chateau's Gero was Best of Breed at the National Specialty in 1978, having also been Best of Sex in 1975. Ch. High Chateau's Androcles was one of their well-known dogs, owned by Bruce Crabb and Winifred Vogel. He was seventh top winning dog in 1979. He was a son of High Chateau's Neptune out of High Chateau's Gwen. Neptune was by High Chateau's Barabas out of Ch. High Chateau's Gerda, and Gwen was by Ch. High Chateau's Invincible out of Joraca's Princess Tahara.

Classes at the American shows are for each sex and divided into Puppy 6-9 months, Puppy 9-12 months, Junior 12-18 months, Bred by Exhibitor, American bred, Open Long-haired, Open Short-haired, Veteran, and Best of Breed, in which all Champions compete against the 'Winners' for the Best of Breed. The best of each sex, other than Champions, is termed the Best of Winners, and it is for this award that points are awarded towards the Championship title, depending on both the area of the show and the number of exhibits. Once a dog has gained the title of Champion it can no longer compete for the Winners points, whereas in Britain a dog can go on winning Challenge Certificates when it is already a Champion. In Europe a class is allocated for Champions in each of the sexes and both types of coat; there are also two sets of Championships in continental Europe – one for the long-haired and one for the short-haired.

Donna Buxton, who owns the Twin Oaks kennels in partnership with her husband Kenneth, is one of the top American St Bernard judges. Their home-bred Ch. Twin Oaks Cinnamon Bear UD was the first Champion UD bitch in the breed, and only the third St Bernard to win all three obedience titles. Since then, the American Kennel Club has added the titles of TDX and OT CH. Many St Bernard breeders in the U.S.A. train their dogs for obedience competitions, and the 1988 Centennial Show had obedience classes scheduled. There are a number of obedience titles which can be attained. The first is Companion Dog (CD), which comprises walking to heel on and off the lead, sit, down, stand and recall. Companion Dog Excellent (CDX) brings time into consideration, as well as jumping and retrieving. Utility Dog (UD) entails walking to heel off the lead, jumping and scent discrimination from non-verbal commands. For the Tracking Dog (TD) title the dog must follow a quarter-mile trail, the scent being a half hour old, and for Tracking Dog Excellent (TDX) the dog must follow a half-mile trail, the scent being three hours old. Obedience Trial Champion (OT CH) is the highest honour to attain in the obedience world, and only dogs that have attained the Utility Dog (UD) title may compete for this award.

Ch. Mountain Scout CDX, owned by Harold Jarvis was the first St Bernard to win

*The Southern Californian Show 1990. Winners Dog (left) Beau Mars Stamp of
Approval.*   *Munro*

an obedience title in the late thirties. Am. & Can. Ch. Nicklus of Hyden Am. & Can.
UD, owned by John Cox, was the first St Bernard to achieve both the American and
Canadian Utility title. He was also placed third in the World Championship Weight
Pull, pulling 3,300 pounds. The World Top dogs of Glen Williams from Alaska are
well-known for their weight-pulling feats. In 1974 World Top's Kashwitna v Thor,
owned by Frances Good, pulled 6,000 pounds fifteen feet in fifteen seconds (weight-
pulling is done on sledges or with carts). The St Bernard Club of America held its
first annual Weight Pull on June 16th 1988. There were three classes scheduled,
according to the dog's weight. The class for dogs weighing less than 125 pounds
was won by Sebring's Summer Breeze, owned by Dvorak, weighing 118lbs. Breeze
pulled 1,940 pounds in sixteen seconds. She also won the prize for best percentage
weight pull of the day, pulling 16.4 times her own weight. The 125-150 pound class
was won by Murphy's Ch. Sweetholm's M-S Contessa, weighing 135 pounds; she
pulled 1,660 pounds in twelve seconds. The over 150 pounds class went to Glen
William's Ch. World Top's Brutus von Opdyke, who weighed 174 lbs, and pulled
1,940 pounds in 7.4 seconds. The runner-up in this class was Birkby's Ch. Heaven's
High Dream Baby, weighing 159 lbs, he equalled the weight pulled by Brutus but it
took him sixteen seconds. On the same day the first annual draft tests were held.
Seven dogs were entered, and two passed all parts of the test to become official draft
dogs. They were Mar Ed Asco's Colt Forty Five CD, owned by Mr and Mrs Marker
of Salkum, Washington, and sired by Ch. Asco v Langerhang out of Dustyacre's
Magic Marker CDX; and Mar Wil's Markus von Hyden CD, owned by John Cox of

Pat Muggleton awarded Best in Show to Ch. Sweetholm's Gad About at the 1990 Southern Californian Specialty. *Munro*

Seattle, Washington. This dog was bred by Camilla Thorne, sired by Ch. Opdyke's Bo Jangles out of Ch. Warwil's DD. The test involved some advanced obedience exercises performed while pulling a draft apparatus – all exercises were lead-free. The club's first annual tracking test had been held the previous day, and of the three dogs entered only Mar-Wil's Markus von Hyden completed the course and gained his tracking title.

Back in 1972 Colorado's St Bernard Rescue Unit was formed. It provided the Rocky Mountains with a team of qualified working dogs, consisting of individually owned and handled dogs trained to work as an organised unit. As well as being trained for avalanche rescue, as their ancestors were many years ago, the unit also works with ground searches.

We all recently visited California, which gave us a first-hand look at the St Bernards there. Pat judged the St Bernard Club of Southern California's Specialty Show in February 1990, and awarded Best in Show to Ch. Sweetholm's Gad About.

He was bred by Marilyn Murphy, sired by Ch. Sweetholm's Dakota von Astro out of Almshaus Just a Breeze, and owned by William and Shirley Tsagris of the Kings Row kennels. Best Winners was the short-haired dog, Beau Mar's Stamp of Approval, bred and owned by Joyce and Richard Simmons of the Beau Mar's kennels. He was handled by William (Billy) Buell. Winners Bitch went to the long-haired L.T.'s Janelle, bred and owned by Styron and Bertha Pool. She was by Ch. Lenwardof's Garfield out of Ch. L.T.'s Aynaquandra. Sky Meadows Zodiak, bred and owned by Jack and Dolores Landgraf, won the Open long-haired dog class. Best Puppy was Subira's Nadia, bred by Chantel and Mark Cutter and owned by Betty Omohundro, Sandra Rodrigo and Judith Buell, and handled by Billy Buell. The Subira kennel also won Bred by Exhibitor dogs, in partnership with Tony Valdez. The St Bernard Club of San Diego's Specialty Show was held the day prior to the Californian club's show. American clubs in close proximity often hold their shows alongside each other – there will sometimes be four shows in four successive days – and many exhibitors travel in motor homes and stay in these for the duration of the shows. Unfortunately, Pat was not allowed to visit this show by American Kennel Club regulations, as a judge of a show may not visit a show of the same breed, immediately prior to the judging engagement.

Michael was luckier when he judged the Californian Show the following year, as this show was held first. He awarded Best of Breed to Echo's Keets von Yondo, a large, impressive long-haired dog, who had been absent the previous year. Keets was bred and owned by Carol Thom of the Echo's kennels, which have been successful for many years. Keets was sired by Ch. Benbarron's Yondo von Gizer, the beautiful short-haired dog who has sired some excellent stock. Yondo started his show career winning Best Puppy at the National Specialty in 1985. He went on to win Best of Breed at the Specialty for two years in succession, in 1986 and 1987. Keets' dam was Ch. Echo's A-Me von Zipcode. In the ring Keets was handled by Billy Buell. Ch. Echo's Just Me von Yondo, also owned and bred by Carol and Wallace Thom, was in the top ten in 1979, and Ch. Echo's Citation von Bonus, bred by the Thoms and owned by Donald Dube and Dr Rodos, was in the top ten in 1975. Michael's Best Bitch was the aforementioned Hanaethorp Bea, owned by Mike Sherman. Pat's Winners Dog in 1990 won the short-haired dog class and was Reserve Winners Dog. Mike's Reserve Winners Bitch was Big Foots Legacy v Sky Meadows, owned by Dolores and Jack Landgraf of Sky Meadows kennels. The St Bernard Club of California is run by the Buells and Sandra Rodrigo of the Subira kennels. The St Bernard Club of San Diego is run by Ray and Minnie Horlings and Michael Sherman. Ray Horlings is the American Club representative to the World Union.

Many of the American breeders visit and import stock from the rest of Europe, but few have been imported from England in the post-war years. A Bernmont smooth, some Burtonswoods dogs and two Swindridge bitches went to live in the U.S.A., but the majority of imports have come from Holland, Germany and the Soccorso kennels in Italy.

Further information on St Bernard clubs and active breeders can be obtained from the American Kennel Club Customer Service, 580 Centerville Drive, Raleigh, North Carolina 27606. The telephone number is 919 233 9767

CANADA

Mr and Mrs R.A. Mollard started the Lake Manitou kennels in Saskatchewan in the late twenties. The kennels were sold in the late forties to Mr and Mrs G. Gill, who had been previously employed by the Mollards. The Gills kept the kennels until the late sixties when they retired through ill health. However, the best known of the old Canadian Kennels was the Kobi's kennels of Charles Cawker. His kennel was previously called Charlinore, and prior to that du Grand St Bernard, which is the name of the Hospice's kennels in Switzerland. Mr Cawker imported the magnificent short-haired Can. & Am. Ch. Kobi v Steinerhof, who was by Rasko v d Roth out of Hulder v Schmeiderain, and the long-haired Negus v d Markthalle by Sieger Roy von Neu Habsburg out of Bella v Lotten. Another male import was Elio v Enziwiggerstrand, sired by Int. Ch. Castor v Leberberg out of Est v Rigihand. Some of the bitches imported by Mr Cawker include Erla de la Theurre, sired by Edi v Grafensteiner out of Carla du Grand St Bernard (Swiss), and the short-haired Asta v Burgenstock, by Int. Ch. Castor v Leberberg out of Cara von Sauliamt. Kobi was the sire of several Beau Cheval Champions including Ch. Beau Cheval's Tablo la Mardoug, Ch. Beau Cheval's Mia La Mardoug, Ch. Beau Cheval's Gard la Mardoug, Ch. Beau Cheval's Banks la Mardoug and Ch. Beau Cheval's Bella la Mardoug. He was also the sire of Can. & Am. Ch. Lady Geneva of Shagg Bark and Shagg Barks Grand Kobi. Am. & Can. Ch. Alpine Acre Baron of Shagg Bark was sired by Grand Kobi, and he went on to sire several top winners. Ch. Charlinore's Grand Ursula came from Kobi and the imported Asta. Many du Grand St Bernard stock that are found in the ancestry of today's top winners originate from Erla du Grand St Bernard – a daughter of Erla de la Theurre and Kobi. The young Erla was mated to the imported Negus and among the resulting progeny were Countess, Dixie and Freda – all du Grand St Bernard. Negus also produced excellent stock for the Shagg Bark kennels in Connecticut, when he changed hands at the age of seven. Elio sired Can. Ch. Kobi's Grand Count III, Am. & Can. Ch. Kobi's Grand Tyras, Am. & Can. Ch. Kobi's Grand Wachter and Can. Ch. Rocharest's Ensign. Am. & Can. Ch.

Kobi von Steinerhof is in the ancestry of many of today's top winners.

Mrs Eda Mitchell bought Bernmont Tania of Berngarth from Pat and her mother in 1964. This bitch became a Canadian Champion at eleven months of age, and by the time she was fourteen months old she was the top winning Saint in Canada with eight Best of Breeds, four Best of Opposite Sex awards and five Group placings. She was born in June 1964, sired by Bernmont Christcon St Rajar out of Bernmont Cornagarth St Angela. Mrs Mitchell got her prefix Berngarth from the combination of the Bernmont and Cornagarth bloodlines in her stock. Mrs Mitchell later returned to England. One of the leading kennels in Canada today is the Bergwacht's owned by Karl and Mary Winter, who are based in British Columbia. They used Sanctuary Woods bloodlines for their foundation stock. Am. & Can. Ch. Bergwacht's Far West, who is by Am. & Can. Ch. Bergwacht's Buccaneer out of Sanctuary Woods Gem of the U.S.A., won Best of Breed at the American St Bernard Club's National Specialty in 1979. At one time he belonged to a British Coumbia Park Ranger who patrolled the outback cabins on foot, and sometimes the dog and his master walked forty miles a day. This remarkable St Bernard combined all that is best in the breed in terms of looks and character, and he once won an award for bravery after taking on a black bear that was menacing a child. Karl Winter, who is a mountain climber, often fits a Saint with panniers carrying rescue gear. He has found that St Bernards are still sure-footed and do not lose the trail – even when it is covered with snow. In fact, both Canada and America now use the St Bernard for its original work as a rescue dog, while in its native Switzerland the St Bernard has been replaced by German Shepherd Dogs and helicopters. The Bergwacht kennel has been in existence for some twenty years, and Ch. Bergwacht's Dolomite and Ch. Bergwacht's Don Juan v Ranier are just two of their highly successful dogs. Mary Winter is an artist, and she often features St Bernards in her work.

The Heldisaint kennels from Alberta are owned by Marion L. Buckton, and her foundation stock came from the Bergwacht kennels. The Heidisaint Champions include Ch. Heidisaint's St Andrew, Ch. Heidisaint's Kavalier v Jura and Ch. Heidisaint's Macho. The Canadian stock today carries the bloodlines of many of the leading kennels in the U.S.A., and the Kennebank kennels of Joost and Pat Postma own an excellent son of Yondo – Ch. Benbaron's Abraham von Yondo. His sire, Am. & Can. Ch. Yonda von Gizer, the dual National Specialty winner of 1986 and 1987 is owned by the Beniger family, based in Ontario.

Ch. Bernmont Tania of Berngarth, a top winning St Bernard in Canada in the Sixties.

Henry Schumacher (1831-1903): the leading breeder and exhibitor of St Bernards in Switzerland.

Chapter Eight

THE ST BERNARD WORLDWIDE

The St Bernard clubs of the world, with the exception of Britain, have been united by the World Union of St Bernard Clubs for the last quarter of a century. It was the brainchild of the late Albert de la Rie of Holland, and latterly Switzerland. Each year one of the member countries hosts the World Union of St Bernard Clubs Show. It has been held in Germany, Italy, Holland, Belgium, Denmark and France. The show normally attracts an entry of around two hundred dogs from the member countries, with occasional entries from America, Spain and Austria. The reunification of Germany has meant that exhibitors from the Eastern bloc can now participate, and there were entries from what was formerly East Germany at the WUSB show in Denmark in 1990.

Sweden and Norway are governed by quarantine restrictions, although these are not as stringent as those in the U.K. Both countries are only allowed to import dogs from rabies-free countries such as Britain. Finland also has quarantine restrictions – although an exhibitor got special permission to attend the Danish WUSB. There is no restriction on taking a dog into Europe, other than it being vaccinated against rabies at least thirty days prior to entry, but in the case of British dogs, they cannot return home, unless they have six months in quarantine. As a result, British participation is minimal, although we have visited the WUSB shows as onlookers for several years. There are usually eight judges from the member countries, and two judges from different countries are allocated to each class. All eight judges are then involved in judging Best in Show. This can lead to difficulties, and there have been times when it has taken a considerable time for the judges to reach agreement. When the WUSB was first formed it was decided that the president should come from Switzerland, as that was the original home of the St Bernard. The first president was Hans Zimmerli, the last Swiss president was Peter Schmidlin, and the present president is Herr Ko de Graf from Holland.

EUROPE

SWITZERLAND

Everyone thinks of the Hospice of the Great St Bernard as being the first home of our dogs, but in fact, many were bred in the valleys and many centuries ago the monks of the Hospice went down to the valleys to select dogs for their work in the mountains. The Swiss St Bernard Club was founded in 1884, at which time the leading breeder was Henry Schumacher. In 1887, in Zurich, Dr. Th. Kunzli was the main instigator in getting the Swiss Breed Standard accepted by all countries, with the exception of Britain. The first recorded show was held in Berne in 1871, when Schumacher won most of the prizes with Barry II, Sultan II and Favorite II. There were twenty-seven St Bernards registered in the first Swiss Stud Book. The next recorded show was held ten years later in Zurich, and there were two hundred St Bernards present. The first prize went to Bello, owned by the Kennel Club of Aarburg. There were no affixes at this time, and it was common practice to add the owner's surname to the dog's name. The next show, held in 1882, was organised by the Kennel Club of Aarburg, and the first prize was withheld. Bello, the previous year's winner, was given second prize, along with three other dogs – all named Barry. The leading breeder, Schumacher, was the judge the following year, and he did not give a first prize to any of the sixty-five entrants, although he awarded several second prizes. Looking back today, it is difficult to work out whether the judges were harsh in their assessments, or whether it was a true reflection of the quality of the dogs. We do know that there was a considerable amount of indiscriminate breeding at this time in order to satisfy the demand for St Bernards – particularly from the British.

The 1884 show, held in Basle, had fewer entries, with only twenty-eight dogs competing. Two first prizes were awarded for short-haired dogs, with honours going to Apollo, owned by Schumacher, and Belline owned by Bernhard. In long-coats

Three St Bernards from the famous Sauliamt kennels.

three first prizes were awarded to Wurf (Merion), Bello (Dr Kunzli), and Barry (Tuch Schmid). By 1890 Dr Kunzli had between seventy and a hundred dogs in his kennels. Other well-known breeders of the time were E. Bauer, R. Egger, Siber, and Major Blosch. Carl Steiner was beginning to make his name in the Swiss show scene. He changed his prefix from v Arth to von Rigi, and continued to breed St Bernards until his death in the early forties. His son then took over the kennels, but unfortunately Carl Jr. died soon afterwards. The kennel had many excellent short-haired dogs, and several were exported to Britain and the U.S.A. There were von Rigi dogs in the pedigree of the first Bernmont Saints in the U.K. – Ch. Yew Tree St Christopher was a grandson of Berndean Prinz von Rigi. F. Mannus of the Gutsch kennel was also influential in this formative period of the breed in Switzerland. Steinegger, of the v Uto kennel, also bred many outstanding dogs in the early years of the 20th century.

By the turn of the century, show entries were poor and the soundness of the dogs was being criticised. There had been much demand for the exceptionally large dogs, and as we know today, it is not so easy to breed a big, sound dog as it is to breed a small, sound dog. Some Swiss breeders were worried that heads were becoming too Pug-like, with too short a muzzle. There were three shows in Switzerland in 1903, and two of them had entries of over a hundred St Bernards. For some reason most of the well-known breeders were missing from the show at Langenthal, and many of the dogs that were entered did not even have a pedigree. There was an entry of one hundred and fifteen at Zurich in 1906, and over a hundred entries at Langenthal in 1908, where the Steinegger's Uto kennels took many of the prizes. In 1908 the Swiss St Bernard Club ruled that the dogs owned by club members could only serve bitches that were registered in the Swiss Stud Book. The result of this was that many breeders started to register their bitches, which they had failed to do in the past. Entries at the shows remained fairly static over the next few years: 1911 – 86, 1912 – 91, and 76 in 1913. For the first time there were more long-haired dogs being entered than short-haired. The breakdown of show entries over ten years was 445 short-haired compared with 441 long-haired.

By 1914 breeders such as Leuenberger of the Jura kennels and Giavina of Belmont were beginning to make their mark. The other kennels that were prominent in this era were Oenz (A.Wurthrich) and Neu Habsburg (Charles Baehler). Baehler's daughter, Mrs Simone Bammater continued the kennels for many years, and judged until her death in 1991. The bitch Brita von Salmegg, imported from Switzerland to Britain by Mrs Dixon and Dr Westell, was a daughter of Sieger Roy von neu Habsburg. The Bernmont kennels had a son from this bitch – Bernmont Fernebrandon Ajax – sired by Ch. Christcon St Jeremy.

At the 1925 shows at Berne and Basle there were ninety-eight St Bernards entered, and only seventeen of these were given the award 'excellent' (all dogs entered at continental shows are graded: excellent, very good, good or mediocre). This was the first time that the famous Zwing Uri kennels, owned by Charles Sigrist, were represented. Cornagarth Marshall van Zwing Uri was the first post-war import to Britain to become a Champion. Cornagarth Recorder of Bernmont, a son of Marshall, was purchased by the Bernmonts in the early fifties. Hans Zimmerli started the v d Markthalle kennels in 1930, at the same time that Hans Schiffer established the Sauliamt kennels. Otto Steiner, not to be confused with Carl Steiner of the v Rigis, started the Lotten Kennels, and Walter Urben started the Melina kennels. The long-haired variety had now taken over as the most popular, and in the thirties there were twice as many long-haired registered as short-haired.

The breed suffered a severe decline during the Second World War: in 1940 there were only a hundred St Bernards registered, and this fell to its lowest ebb in 1941 with only thirty-one registrations. During these war years the notable breeders were

Carl Steiner Jr. (v Rigi), Sigrist (v Zwing Uri), Grossenbacher (v d Lueg), K. Fredli (Bornfeld) and W. Urben (Melina). The death of Mannus and Giavina in the early forties brought an end to the great Guttsch and Belmont kennels. The Huttwil kennel of Walter Jordi was the only new kennel of note at this time. The Oenz kennels were dominant in the late forties, and the Liebiwil kennels of W. Wurstemberger was a new name on the scene. The Sauliamt kennel name was continued in the early fifties by Eduard Rodel, and it was from this source that Mrs Clare Bradley bought Tello v Sauliamt in the sixties. This dog won two CCs, but he never got his English title. The original Swindridge Saints were descended from Tello. By the early fifties the breed was beginning to re-establish itself, and two hundred St Bernards were registered. The Hospice of the Grand St Bernard and the Zwing Uri kennels were dominant amongst the registrations at this time, with Kussnacht, Schmiederain, Schwandenblick, Bachingerhof, and Hanialthus beginning to play a part. In fact some British Saints can be traced to Tyrus v Haniathus. Cargo von Leberberg, a son of Tyras v Hanialthus was the grandsire of the Birkenkopf litter, which was born in quarantine in England. The mid-fifties saw the start of the Leberberg kennel, owned by F. Hurzeler, and the Rigihang kennels, owned by Mrs Muller.

Registrations dropped to one hundred and sixteen in 1957, with twenty-two of these from the Sauliamt kennels and twenty from the Hospice. The Burgenstock kennel of Eduard Bachmann started in the early sixties, and by 1963 registrations had gone up to three hundred and nineteen – thirty-nine of these were bred by the Hospice and seventy-six came from the mighty Sauliamt kennels. In 1966 a third of the total registration figure of three hundred and sixty were Sauliamts. The Malters kennels of Herr Sidler and the Merlotreu kennels are now important names on the Swiss scene. Ch. Anton von Hoffli was sired by Bruno v Leberberg out of Cita v Rigihang. He was bought by Dr Antonio Morsiani for his Soccorso kennels. Another Swiss dog owned by the Soccorso kennels was Ch. Joggi v Linksmader, a grandson of Ch. Castor v Leberberg and Ch. Roy von Neu Habsburg. The Swiss bitch, Ch. Connie v Rheinsberg was another Swiss import and was one of the foundation bitches of the Soccorso kennels.

The Swiss St Bernard club held its centenary show in 1984 and a total of two hundred and seventy-one dogs were entered from many countries in Europe, plus Canada and South Africa. There was a banquet the evening before the show, which is the custom with the large Championship events on the continent attracting an international entry. The Sauliamt kennel was represented, along with Hans Jost, (Dorneggutsch), Berta Katheriner (von den Dornen), Kohli (von Anet), Karl Mehli (Hegibachli), Ernst Kientsch (Schweizerhof), Peter Schmidlin (von der Moesa), Peter Buckingham (Altoggenburg), Lisette Gloor Laube (Merlos) and Victor and

Margret Burri, whose Schwitzer Landi kennel was possibly one of the largest on the continent since the earlier days of the Sauliamts. Roland Hans of the Gnod prefix was one of the judges at the German centenary in 1991, and the Swiss breeders are still widely respected, even though the Swiss St Bernard does not have the influence on overseas stock that it used to in the breed's formative years.

GERMANY

The St Bernhard Klub was founded in Munich in 1891, and the greatest concentration of St Bernard breeders was in Bavaria. The German club is by far the strongest St Bernard club in Europe. In 1892 it established the St Bernard 'Zuchtbuch' to keep a record of all the St Bernards in the country, and their pedigrees. In the U.K., and in most other countries, registrations are controlled by the national Kennel Club, but the German club handles all registrations for the breed to this day, and it even organises the breed classes at the general Championship shows, under the auspices of the V. D.H. (the German Kennel Club).

Prior to the foundation of the German St Bernard Club there had been much interest in the breed, and some authenticated records were desperately needed. As early as 1882 breeders were having difficulty in tracing the ancestry of stud dogs, as the great demand for St Bernards at the time had resulted in some breeders selling inferior stock, of dubious background, for financial gain. The breed was considered to be the ideal companion and watchdog, particularly favoured by clergymen who went out on lonely missions – the St Bernard was considered to have a better temperament than the Great Dane.

Some of the early St Bernard breeders were: Dr Caster of Rheingau, Prince Albrech of Solms-Braunfels, Mr Hartenstein and Lieutenant Fink of Berlin. Prince Albrecht owned the Wolfsmuhle kennels, and they were one of the largest on the continent. His first import was Courage, a beautiful dog, who won first prize at the 1878 Berlin show, and at four other shows in Holland and England – quarantine regulations were not introduced to England until the twenties. Courage was said to be thirty-five inches tall, and weighed one hundred and forty pounds. By present day standards, this does not seem very heavy, compared with the dog's height, but St Bernards at this time tended to be lighter in bone. Courage sired only a few litters, but Prince Albrecht kept the line going by breeding Courage II out of Hedwig by Courage, and Courage III out of Alp by Courage II. Courage III was very much like his grandsire, but not as tall. Prince Albrecht also owned Gessler, and the bitches Bernina II, Hospice and Berna II, who had been imported from Switzerland along with Alp. When Courage II was mated to Berna II she produced exceptional stock, and so the mating was repeated. Each litter produced puppies of good conformation with good heads, and they were well marked. Some of the Wolfsmuhle dogs were sold to Switzerland, as good stud dogs were in short supply, as all the best dogs had been sold by the Swiss to English and Russian breeders at huge prices. Dr Caster suggested that several fanciers should join together to buy an outstanding female and breed it to one of the best studs in England. At the time there were mainly long-haired dogs in Germany, and they were of inferior quality compared to the short-haired Saints, because they carried too much Newfoundland blood.

There were thirty-six long-haired St Bernards listed in the 1882 Hannover show, as well as forty dogs described as Newfoundlands, but as they had no pedigrees they were put into the same Group. In fact, many of the entrants at the show were considered to be Leonbergers – large long-haired dogs of no known pedigree, descendants of large mongrels. They had good bodies, but no type bearing resemblance to the St Bernard. The first prize was awarded to Cadwallader – a large dog, with a good head and muzzle, and excellent colouring. He was a reddish colour with white markings; in these early times many Saints were of a light yellow tinge. The second prize went to the Prince of Solms Gessler. This dog also had a beautiful head and a noble expression, but he had grey colouring on a white background. Neither Courage nor Courage II were placed at the show, although several dogs of the dubious background were. Dishonest judging was suspected, but not proven. The judge was an Englishman.

Among the other early breeders were Herr Hartenstein of the Plavia kennels, who imported several Swiss dogs – the best was Prinz of Burgdorf; Adelbert Sohst of Hamburg bred many Saints from his Hammonia Kennels; Dr Calaminus of Langendiebach was the first president of the St Bernard Club; W. and E. Guretzy of Cornitz, Berlin, Dr Toll of Mulheim, Herr Kempel of Urach, Herr Burger of Leonberg and Pingerra from Munich were all active in the breed, although Pingerra's Bavarian kennel was reputed to breed for quantity rather than quality. One of the best of the old breeders was Herr G. Schmitbauer of Munich, who founded his Munichia kennel from several good imports from Switzerland. They included Herakles (31), Saentis, Barry (49), Berna, Troja (146), Priest (218), Meta II (615), and Barry Frauenfeld (213). Ch. Munichia Lord, Ch. Munichia Pierette, Munichia Ivo, Munichia Rival and Munichia Sparta are the foundation stock of most of today's German Saints.

New breeders were coming into the St Bernard world, and they included Bubet of Mehlem, Guerteler of Munich, Kohn of Ravensburg and latterly Augsburg, Boppel of Canstatt, and Max Nather of Munich. Nather owned Wodans Barry (1091), one of the great St Bernards of the past, plus Wodans Rasko (1409), Wodan v Schwabung

Antje von St Florian, World Junior winner, (left) and two kennel companions.
Owned by Erika Janes and Heinz Kalscheur.

(701), Wodans Saturn (1969), Wodans Stella (2982) and Wodans Heidi. These dogs are descended from the Hospiz, Deppeler and Munichia strains. In 1894 there were three hundred and one St Bernards registered in the Stud Book – one hundred and seventy-five short-haired and one hundred and twenty-six long-haired – and the St Bernard was the most popular dog in Germany. The club stated that its aims were to improve type, body, size, colour and markings.

Mr Kempel of the Urach kennels tried to breed dogs of good temperament. His kennels were one of the best of the time, and they included Athos, Tell, Flora v Basel and her daughter Gemma, Blanka Urach and her son Ch. Barry Urach, plus Norma Urach who produced Ch. Wotan v lberfield and Ada v Plankstadt. He later bought Jupiter out of Tuerk and Liaume from the Hospice. Other breeders of this era were Bostelmann of Mechelfield, Mrs Deichmann of Mehlem, Fehn of Erlangen, Groos of Wiesbaden, Hoffmann of Hannover, Krause of Dresden, Langfried of Obergerlachsheim, Countess Larisch of Munich, Latz of Euskirchen, Mrs Nickau of Gohlis, near Leipzig, Probst of Munich, Teufel of Tuttlingen and Wachendorf of Steglitz. Many great kennels were founded at the end of the nineteenth century, the

Sando v Geutenreuth taking honours at Germany's Centennial Show in 1991.

majority of which were in Bavaria, in the south of Germany. The Prince of Solms, who had imported Barry Braunfels from Switzerland and several dogs from England, died in 1901 and this marked the end of his Wolfsmuhle kennels. Herr Hartenstein of Plauen, who had also bought many imports, the best of which was Prinz v Burgdorf, also came to end at this time.

A number of new kennels were started at the turn of the century and these included von Moeckern, von Kronental, von Dessau, von Langenstein, von Dusseldorf and von Altona. This last kennel was started by Ludwig Kasten and his descendants have continued breeding St Bernards throughout the century – his son Georg of the von Norden kennels, his grandson Herbert of the von Izola kennels and his great granddaughter Martina are all active in the breed.

There were two outstanding stud dogs in the south of Germany, these were litter brothers Barry v Fuerth and Ch. Troubadour v Dusseldorf. At this time there were many poor quality dogs with narrow heads and weak muzzles, incorrect tail carriage, and in general, the dogs were too small. At the end of the first decade of the new century some of the best dogs were Ch. Wola v Stadtilm, Prinz v Stadtilm, Ch. Nonne v Fuerstenfeld, Ch. Argos v d Hammerburg, Ch. Barry v Goepingen, Ch. Prinz v Goeppingen, Lola v Bernhardinerheim and Ch. Thalattas. The von Falkenstein kennels owned by Herr Zillinger started just before the outbreak of the

First World War. His dog Ch. Theo's Minka v Falkenstein was mated to his imported bitch, Toja Guetsch and produced many fine dogs including Ch. Kora v Falkenstein and Ch. Wanda v Falkenstein. Sadly, during the war numbers dwindled considerably due to shortage of food, and only the very best specimens were retained.

After the war Herr Kasten started to look for a large stud dog, as there were no dogs of sufficient size in the north of Germany. Eventually he bought Ch. Xenos v Taubertal from Bavaria. He was sired by Ch. Kavalier v Grossglockner out of Ch. Leda v Taubertal. Ch. Xenos improved the breed in the north enormously. Some of his Champion progeny were Ch. Grief v d Helenenburg and Ch. Gretel v d Helenenburg, Ch Nelson v Falkenstein and Ch. Dieter v Norden. Dieter was later sold to Southern Germany. Altona's Alf won many prizes, but unfortunately he died when he was still young. He was sired by Xenos's half-brother, Ch. Aegir v d Scheerenburg, another son of Ch. Kavalier v Grossglockner. The Grossglockner kennels were started just before the outbreak of the first World War by Hans Glockner, and several outstanding dogs bore the Grossglockner prefix. These included Armin v Grossglockner (sire of Ch. Bernd v Mitterfels), Art v Grossglockner, Baer v Grossglockner (a son of Mr Glockner's Rigi v Hessen), Dumar v Grossglockner, Rasco v Grossglockner, Wito v Grossglockner (a son of Ch. Fritz Drei Lilian) and Zeno v Grossglockner (a son of Eros Guetsch) – Fritz and Eros were descendants of the Swiss dog Emir Jura. Both Ch. Esbo v Grossglockner and Ch. Kavalier v Grossglockner made names for themselves in America where they were taken by Mr Fleischli.

Despite the difficulties encountered, a number of kennels survived through the war. They were von den drei Lilien, founded by Johann Wagner and taken over by his son Hans, vom Grossglockner (Hans Glockner, Diesenhofen), vom Rheinland (Peter v Itter, Dusseldorf), vom Taubertal (Hans Meyer, Neumarkt), von Freudenfels (Freudling, Obereichstadt), von Alsatia (Bauer, Ittigheim), von Elberfeld, von der Vorstadt (Klee, Hannau), von Crimmitschau (Richard Ehrler, Krimmitschau), von Hemphorn (Hermann Lippert, Berlin), von Mitterfels, von Norden (Kasten). In 1923 the German St Bernard Club had 750 members divided between eight area groups. Some of the best dogs were: Ch. Tangua v Rheinland, Ch. Castor v Freudenfels, Ch. Tasso I v Freudenfels, Ch. Rigi v Hessen, Ch. Estor v Taubertal, Ch. Elmire v Rheinland and Ch. Bernd v Mitterfels.

In 1934 the St Bernard was the tenth most popular dog in Germany. The German club set the minimum age at which a stud dog could be used at two years, and a brood bitch had to be a minimum age of twenty months. The bitch could not be used more than once a year, and only six puppies raised from one litter were eligible for registration in the Stud Book. Mr de la Rie was particularly impressed by the dogs from the Falkenstein kennels at the 1935 World Show in Frankfurt. There were seventy-nine St Bernards entered – sixty-one long-haired and eighteen short-haired. However, this compared poorly with the one hundred and fifty-seven Saints entered in Munich in 1907. The German dogs at this time were of exceptional quality, and only the very best of the Swiss dogs could compete against them.

In 1937 the Nazis tried to interfere with the breeding of St Bernards. They changed the name of the St Bernhard Club to 'Fachschaft fur Berhardiner', and an SS magazine *Das Schwarze Korps* tried to convince their readers of the undesirable qualities of the St Bernard. They said that the shape of the St Bernard's head and eyes indicated viciousness, and they printed an article stating that a girl had been torn to pieces by a vicious St Bernard which had to be shot. The Nazis also stopped the titles of Club Champion and International Champion being awarded in the breed. However, at the beginning of the war the Nazis decided to train St Bernards as rescue and first aid dogs for the mountain units. Registrations fell during the war years, although some of the German breeders still carried on, even though dogs were being bartered for food or anything else useful. In 1945 when Nazism was defeated the German breeders renamed their club as the St Bernhard Club.

One of the best known kennels to survive the second world war was the Bismarkturm kennels owned by Alois Schmid, who died at the age of ninety-two in 1988. The kennel is still in existence, breeding excellent St Bernards, in the ownership of his grandson, Hans Wiebauer. Henry Gardes's was another new kennel that kept going through the war, and the Kasten family are still breeding St Bernards to this day. Maly Schmitt started the Bretano kennel, later known as Bretan Schloss, in 1946. Some of the good stud dogs available in 1949 were Monch von Werdenfels, bred by Christian Wagner; Dieter, Elmon, Falko and Jago v Bismarkturm, all bred by Alois Schmid; and Edel and Elmo v Staufenbrunnen, bred by Friedrich Straub. The first recognised judging list after the war consisted of twelve names: Eduard Block, Berlin; Ludwig Deinzer, Munich; A. Freundling, Garmisch; Hans Glockner, Franz Hrachowina, Munich; Ludwig Kasten, Hamburg; Fr. Krossing, Hamburg; Hans Kunzmann, Sprendlingen; Fr. Links, Leipzig; Franz Stobe, Stadtsteinach; Fr. Straub, Goppingen; and Martin Wolf, with Georg Kasten joining the number in 1950. By the end of 1953 the club had over 400 members.

In 1956 at the World Show in Dortmund the winners were Astor von Heldenhof, Belisar v Dornegusch, P'adda v d Dreitor-Alpspitz, and Bella v Werdenfels. Otto Jacob started his St Klara Kloster kennels in 1958, and St Klara Kloster dogs came to Britain in the early seventies. In 1959 Otto Ulrich started the vom Birkenkopf kennels. A litter from a Birkenkopf bitch was born in quarantine in England in 1969. Jorg von Delm was the male winner at the Bundessiegerschau show in 1961, the bitch winner was Adda v Lippingau. At the 1963 Bundessieger show a group from the Rotenkreuz kennels of Joseph Stecker was best out of sixty in the breeders group. By 1964 the club had 800 members, divided among ten area groups. Sando v Bismarkturm was the winner at the Bundessieger show in November 1964. Dr Morsiani of Italy thought that this was the best St Bernard he had seen since the war, and he bought several Bismarkturm dogs for his own kennels. The 1965 winners were Arko von Georgihof and Zahra von Rotenkreuz. By the seventies the club had over 1000 members.

At the World Show at Austria in 1976 three of the winners were German: the long-haired Asterix v Paffenwinkel and Fara v d Freien Reichstadt, and the short-haired Greif v Bayerischen Wald (this dog is the grandfather of our South African import, Alpenheim Ernest). In 1981 the short-haired Antje von St Florian, won the world junior Sieger in Dortmund. Antje was the dam of our Dascha von St Florian, bred by Erika Janes and Heinz Kalscheuer. The world Sieger short-haired winners were Ella v Rotzenberg and Lord v Norfbach; the long-haired winners were Zuleika v Rosenkeller and Boss v Torpedostadt. There were 162 St Bernards entered at the club show in 1981. Best Bitch was Debby v Schloss Morsbroich and Best Dog was Asterix v Paffenwinkel. Vestus v d Drei Helmen won the Sieger show in 1986. He was bred by Messrs Mahrlein and Schreiber of the Drei Helmen Kennels. Our English Champion Pankraz v d Drei Helmen was imported from Herr and Frau Mahrlein in 1983.

Herr Schreiber is the current president of the St Bernard Club, which held its centenary at Leverkussen in May 1991. A dinner was held the evening prior to the show, attended by over 300 guests from all over Europe as well as from America. There were 293 dogs entered at the show, and Best in Show was the short-haired Sando von Geutenreuth, owned by Werner and Edith Moser and bred by Reinhold Welsch. The Geutenreuth kennels have bred many top dogs since 1964. The best long-haired was Sando v Stauferland, bred and owned by Wolfgang Braun. The long-haired Champion class winner and second best long-haired dog was Nelson v Bismarkturm, bred by Hans Wiebauer and owned by Gerhard Mayer of the Baronenschloss kennel. He bred many well known dogs under his former prefix of Rosenkeller. Int. Ch. Angie von Irmengrund was the winner of the long-haired 'Ehren' class. The Irmengrund kennels, owned by Heinz Schonleber was founded in 1968 and is now one of the most successful kennels in Germany.

There are a number of St Bernard kennels currently in operation, and some have been active in the breed for many years. They include: Norfbach (J. Titz); Olympiastadt Munchen (Max and Maria Russ); Rickenhein (Thea Riecken); Rotzenberg (Wolfgang Braun); Schloss Morsbroich (Ursula and Gunther Voss);

Kuttenkeule (Otmar Kuttenkeuler); v Aparten Hofen (Marie Therese Schlosser); v d Bedburger Schweiz (Inge and Wolfgang Ketzler, present secretary of the club); von Brammer (Werner and Margret Brammer); von Lowenhof (Helmut and Marlene Low); v d Niederwiesen (Manfred and Brigitte Liedy) – this kennel has some superb short-haired saints; von Rehberg (Herbert Achenbach); von der Birkenalb (Jacob Steiber); and von der Schwarzmuhle (Karl-Georg Woltenhaupt). These are just a few of the many excellent kennels in present-day Germany. The club has around 1200 members, and approximately 100 are from the former East Germany, but unfortunately we have no details of the East German dogs.

ITALY

The Italian St Bernard world is dominated by the Soccorso kennels of Dr Antonio Morsiani, his wife Maria Leda and their two sons, Giovanni and Pier Luigi. Dr Morsiani owned his first St Bernard in 1940 when he was still a child. This was Emir v d Lueg. The name Morsiani and Soccorso are now famous worldwide; his kennels are based on the best of Swiss and German bloodlines, and it has a preference for big dogs. Ch. Anton v Hofli was one of his favourites, standing 34 inches tall and weighing 215lb. Some of his other imports included Ch. Lorenz v Liebiwil and the short-haired bitch Ch. Zenta v Bismarckturm – Dr Morsiani had great admiration for the dogs of the Bismarckturm kennels, owned by Alois Schmidt. Dr Morsiani has bred and campaigned an incredible number of Champions over the years. They include: Ch. Barry v Rickenheim, Int. Ch. Zito del Soccorso and his sister Ch. Zeda del Soccorso, Int. Ch. Falco del Soccorso, Ch. Sando del Soccorso, Ch. Bedley del Soccorso, Ch. Alma del Soccorso, Ch. Elan del Soccorso, Int. Ch. Diana del Soccorso, Ch. Rolando del Soccorso, owned by F. Gardini; Ch. Saturno del Soccorso, owned by Richard Steinberger and Glenn Radcliffe of the Opdyke kennels, U.S.A.; Int. Ch. Fedor del Soccorso (winner of the WUSB show) owned by L. Cassinotti; Ch. Gianna del Soccorso and Ch. Quarro del Soccorso owned by Dr R. Gagliardini; Ch.Yupiter del Soccorso and Ch. Uberto del Soccors owned by Dr Grassi; Ch. Herbert del Soccorso, owned by Nino Venieri; Int. Ch. Vittorio del Soccorso, owned by Emanuele Venieri, Ch. Oscar del Soccorso and Ch. Ulda del Soccorso, both owned by Paolo Valle; Int. Ch. Iago del Soccorso, Ch. Toga del Soccorso, owned by Ri Casagrandi; Ch. Bruno del Soccorso, Int. Ch. Rex del Soccorso (one of the earlier del Soccorso Champions, who was very tall), Ch. Tyras del Soccorso, owned by Manini Luciano; Ch. Vera del Soccorso, and finally, one of the latest champions, Ch. Sofia del Soccorso.

Dr Morsiani has judged the breed all over the world, including the American and

World Ch. Int. Ch. & It. Ch. Zito del Soccorso: 10 Best in Show, 26 Best of Group, 51 Best of Breed. Owned by Dr Antonio Morsiani.

German centenaries. He judged in Britain in 1988. He is president of the Italian St Bernard Club, which is is possibly the wealthiest St Bernard club in Europe. The trophies given at its club shows to each exhibitor entering the show are bigger than most clubs give to the winners. However, the Italian St Bernard club is very enterprising, and they receive a lot of sponsorship for their shows. Pat judged at their club show in 1989, and it was an education to see how events were conducted. The show was held in conjunction with three other breeds, located in the mountains at the Col du Joux, near Saint Vincent. The day before the show, Giovanni Morsiani drove a van, equipped with a loudspeaker at the head of a procession of exhibitors, who walked through the streets of Saint Vincent with their dogs in order to publicise the show. The result was that some four thousand spectators attended the show. The judges were treated in style, staying at a top-class hotel, and there was a banquet the

Deinhard's Madison Avenue. Owned by Kari Augustad.

evening before the show, attended by approximately three hundred people. Entries came from as far afield as Denmark and the U.S.A. Pat judged the bitches and Dr Morsiani judged the males. The Best in Show winner was Ch. Vittorio del Soccorso.

SPAIN

Spain is a relative newcomer to the St Bernard world, and although the breed has developed with imports from Britain and elsewhere in Europe, the Spanish St Bernard Club was formed in the last decade. In 1991 Pat judged its eighth Club Championship Show, and there was an entry of thirty-nine dogs. The club president, Julian Hernandez, and his wife own the Punta Bernados kennels, and they have imported some excellent St Bernards from Denmark, Germany, Austria and Italy. Best in Show, on this occasion, was Deinhard's Madison Avenue, owned by Kari Augustad, who had imported the dog from Sweden. He was bred by Karin Byrevik, sired by Cache Retreat Oscar Wilde out of Nor. and Sw. Ch. Bernegardens Juliana. Kari Augustad originates from Scandinavia herself, but is married to a Spaniard, and she has lived in Spain for many years. She owns the Estepona kennels, named after the town where she lives – and where the show was held. Dogs from the Estepona kennels accounted for the majority of the entries, and apparently only a few of the top-class dogs travel from show to show, and entries are usually confined to local dogs.

The Estepona kennels had two Champion bitches, both imported from Scandinavia – Bernegardens Notre Dame (a sister of Bernegardens J.R. imported into the United Kingdom) and Deinhards Humble Bee Honey, bred by Karin Byrevik, who also bred the Best in Show Deinhards Madison Avenue. Madison is a beautiful dog with a magnificent head, and sound in movement. He came fifth in a class of sixty dogs at the German Centenary show two weeks later. The bitch CAC winner was Lani Blanco, owned and bred by Lene Mikkelsen, sired by Deinhards Debonhair Gentleman out of Alexis de Estepona. The Spanish St Bernard Club has recently joined the World Union of St Bernard Clubs.

FRANCE

It is strange that the French St Bernards have made so little impact on the rest of the world, as geographically it is in a key position, bordering Switzerland, and the Petit St Bernard Pass links Chambery in France with Aosta in Italy. We attended the French St Bernard Club's eighth Championship Show in 1983, and it was interesting to note that, at this time, they had classes for unregistered dogs as well as registered dogs. Madame Brault, the present president, and Madame Deranger, joint owners of the Tomiere kennels, and are the main breeders. They both judge the breed, as does the past president of the club, Monsieur Tessier. Michael and Ann attended the 1991 World Union of St Bernard Club show, which was hosted by the French at Solgne, near Metz. All major wins went to other countries; the Best in Show was won by Ch. Haenethorp Ruben from Holland. Madame Brault won best veteran.

IRELAND

Ireland is the only country to which British dogs can travel without any quarantine regulations, but Southern Ireland (Eire) has its own Kennel Club and shows with a different Championship system. This is similar to the points system used in America; it is based on the number of dogs attending, and an Irish Champion must have at least one five point Green Star in its total. Ireland has its own St Bernard

Club, which holds its own shows. Several of Eire's leading exhibitors travel to England in the hope of achieving dual Championship status, and likewise, some English exhibitors campaign their dogs in Ireland.

Mr A. K. Gaunt used to send some of his youngsters to be reared at the Durrowabbey kennels, owned by Mrs Slazenger, before they came back to England to be campaigned with the Durrowabbey and Cornagarth prefix. Mrs Slazenger had previously lived in England and had shown dogs with the Thornebarton prefix. Mr Walter Berry of Bangor in Northern Ireland, used to breed St Bernards. He bought a dog from the Bernmont kennels in 1966, and a few years later he added a Hollyabbey dog to his kennels. He now judges the breed. Miss Hindes took her Best in Show Crufts winner to Eire and campaigned Ch. Burtonswood Bossy Boots to his Irish Championship. He was the first St Bernard to hold both titles. Miss Hindes then worked closely with Seamus Oates of the Oatfield Kennels, and they produced several English and Irish Burtonswood Champions, as well as English and Irish Champion Oatfield Nero. Ann and Austin Longdoyle won the CC at Crufts in 1988 with English and Irish Ch. Montaryie Galestorm. He was bred by Michael and Marie Maxwell (nee O'Neill), who currently own Ch. Montaryie Fandango, Ch. Montaryie Fernet Branca and Ch. Bernatha Amaryllis. Michael and Ann sold Swindridge Charlotte to Tony Ryan in 1977, and many of the Longdoyle's Zekeyta Champions are descended from this bitch. Pauline Downey won two CCs with Irish Ch. Killin Smooth Floyd, but unfortunately he died before he could get his third CC and his English title, and a short-haired Saint has yet to hold dual Championship status. Pauline is now winning Green Stars with Fastacre High Hope, a daughter of Ch. Pancras v d Drei Helmen of Bernmont.

The most successful kennel to emerge in recent times is the Barnahely kennels, owned by Michael and Geraldine Barry. They currently have six Champions, two of which have both their English and Irish titles: Eng. & Ir. Ch. Ballincollig of Barnahely and Eng.& Ir. Ch. Ballingeary of Barnahely. The Irish Champions are Ch. Glasslyn Malachite, Ch. Shanaduff Lady, Ch. Beauty's Dream and Ch. Montaryie Geldof. Other well-known names in the Irish Saints world include: the Delafreyne kennels of Conor and Kathleen French, owners of Ch. Delafreyne Black Shadow; the Moyrona kennels of Joseph and Frances Moyniham, presently the home of Ch. Sidmonton Saucy Sue (Sidmonton is the prefix of Des and Carol Bone); and Mr William Halliday's Copperbeach Kennels, owner of Irish Ch. Muffin Bernette, who has also won two CCs.

HOLLAND

Perhaps the best known of the old Dutch breeders was Albert de la Rie. He had his first St Bernard in 1916 – Jacques von St Pancras – and owned the Siegfried Kennels. He lived in Switzerland after the Second World War and judged the breed worldwide. He was the man behind the World Union of St Bernard Clubs, as he wanted to bring a uniformity of type to the breed and to promote discussion between breeders. Other early enthusiasts were M. Steensma, D. Lange and P. Attema, who had purchased excellent stock from Switzerland and Germany. Other breeders of de la Rie's era were Mrs Vallette of the v d Hoeve kennels, P. van Tuinen (Oldehove), G. Biesenbos (Nimmenfor), Th. Schmalz (Schager) and van t Rijnland (Kruithof). Mrs Cloo de Vries bred the Fen't Heitelan Saints for many years and she still judges the breed today. In post-war years some new kennels emerged, including the Da Capo kennels owned by Jan Lammers, P. Smeulder (van Beukenhors) and Martin Zwerts (Majoshof), who currently judges the breed internationally.

Michael organised a party of twelve English St Bernard Club members to visit the Winners Show in Amsterdam in 1977. We visited Mr and Mrs van Wyk's van Wykheim kennel, and they had several good quality St Bernards at the time. It was the start of many return visits between the English St Bernard Club and the Hollandsche St Bernard Club, and we have made many friends in Holland. Bram Vervoorn, a former president of the club, currently owns Ch. Dosco van Spruitenbeek, bred by Jan and Stephanie Overbeek. This male was the result of a mating between Gero v Kuttenkeule and Ch. Mariska v d Spruitenbeek. It was after seeing Dosco and his short-haired litter brother, Ch. Bello v d Spruitenbeek, that Pat decided to buy Ilona v d Spruitenbeek from a repeat mating. The breeders retained the short-haired Int. Ch. Beverley v d Spruitenbeek from the same litter. Dosco is the sire of Int. Ch. Undine v The Finch's White Farm, owned and bred by H. Finke, and she was the best long-haired bitch at the German Centenary Show. Another daughter, Eugene v Spruitenbeek, won the open bitch class for Mr and Mrs Overbeek. Eugene's mother is Ch. Sabina v d Spruitenbeek. Ch. Mariska v d Spruitenbeek is from a litter sired by Int. Ch. Astor v Faustenstein out of Bonnie v Irstenjohof. The Faustenstein kennels, owned by Ko and Rie de Graaf, have bred many excellent short-haired Saints. Mr de Graaf is now the president of the World Union of St Bernard Clubs as well as the Hollandsche St Bernard Club. The Irstenjohof kennels are owned by Mr and Mrs Slootjes, who are also well known for their short-haired Saints. Mrs Diane Fawcett bought Esther v Irstenjohof to England and this bitch has been used to inject new blood into her kennels.

Ilona v d Spruitenbeek of Bernmont came into quarantine in England accompanied

Ch. Mariska v d Spruitenbeek. Owned by Jan and Stephanie Overbeek.

by Johan v h Wapen v Capelle, whom Pat bought from the breeder, A. Stuivenberg. Johan was the son of the well-known Int. Ch. Ashbjorn v d Enchial and Ch. Brendy v d Enchial. The Enchial kennels were owned by Peter Kuypers, who worked closely with Mr and Mrs Nelissen Franssen of the Beukeboscke kennels; Int. Ch. Gypsy v t Beukeboschke is probably the most well-known of their dogs. Miriam Nelissen's father, Charles Fransen, was showing Ch. Cuno v Markthalle, bred by Zimmerli of Switzerland, when we first went to Holland. The Fidelta Saints of Hans and Riet Golveringden are making a name for themselves. The kennel won Best in Show in France in 1991 with Ch. Hanaethorp Ruben. Ruben is sometimes handled by Mr Nieuenhuizen, who owns the v h Hoefsvan kennels – another kennel that breeds short-haireds. Sister Estella shows her St Bernards using the v d Estelon prefix. She is a nun, and she keeps the dogs at the hospital where she works. She handles her dogs with one arm, as she lost the other arm when she was doing missionary work. Other kennels in the Netherlands that are active in the show ring include: the v d Rudolfohoeve kennels, owned by Jan and Maria Huisman, the Asheuvel kennels of J. Te Riele, the Oude Maasdyk kennels of van Acht, the v d Roga Horst kennels of the van Bovens, the Shirons Home kennel, owned by the Smiesing family, who imported a bitch from the Topvalley kennels in the early eighties, the long-established Fen't Nylan kennel, owned by Mrs v d Meer, the

Casanen di Cacho kennels of H. Lammers, J. P. A. van der Belt's De Zandkoele kennels, owner of the excellent German import, Ch. Donar v Ochtumdeich, the von Haus Corina kennel of the Feenstra family and the Bakkers Hoeve kennels of Mr C. Bakker.

The Hollandsche St Bernard Club was founded in 1926, and their Championship shows attract entries of nearly two hundred dogs. They last hosted the WUSB show in 1988 when Ch. Hanaethorp Rico was Best in Show and Lammers's Anouk v Casanan di Cacho was Best Opposite Sex. The Hollandsche club holds club days for its members when their dogs are examined by a judge and a commentary is given on them, but they are not placed. This is an excellent idea as it helps to train the young dogs and it gives the novice handler a preview of what to expect at a show. The club also has an excellent obedience demonstration team led by Miriam Nelissen Franssen. An Obedience display is staged at many shows and there was an excellent display at the German Centenary, when the demonstration was led by two dogs pulling a cart.

BELGIUM

The Belgian St Bernard Club was founded in 1972, and on its tenth anniversary it hosted the WUSB show. This was held in conjunction with a general Championship Show at Gent. The main Belgian breeders are: Mr and Mrs Andre de Groote (van Spitzwacht), Mr and Mrs Freddy de Meyer (van't Hoff ter Stein), Mr and Mrs Claude Broeckkaert (vom Sankt Sigismund), Mr and Mrs Willy Degroote (des Grandes Belles), Mr Jef Hensels (van't Bungerhof), Mr Robert de Leet (van de Burggravehoeve), Mr and Mrs Scott-Legros (du Dannybelle), Mr M. de Wit (Mont Jovis), and Mr and Mrs Weber (de L'Hospitalier), who imported a Bernmont bitch in the early eighties. We must not forget the contribution made by the much-loved former president, the late Mr Rene de Mey.

Some of the main winners from Belgium include: Int. Ch. Jack des Grandes Belles, Int. Ch. Isaura van't Hoff ter Steine and Int. Ch. Princes Grace van het Hoefsen. The Belgian Club often holds inter-club matches with the southern section of the Hollandsche Club. They last hosted the WUSB in 1989, when Ch. Hanaethorp Rico won his second WUSB Best in Show.

AUSTRIA

We attended the World Show at Tulln, near Vienna on May 9th 1986, having driven nine hundred miles the previous day! We had already heard of Frau Brigitte Linser of the Fugerhof kennels, as she shows her St Bernards in Italy and other countries, but we knew little of any of the other breeders. Frau Linser kept the CAC for short-haireds in Austria, also winning the Short-haired Open bitch class with Eike vom Fugerhof, later to become an International Champion. Several Fugerhof Saints have won top honours, and they have done particularly well in the short-haired classes in Italy in 1989. Int. Ch. Puma vom Fugerhof, a son of Eike, is owned by E. Moser of Germany. German Ch. Jago vom Fugerhof is owned by Manfred Liedy in Germany, Int. Ch. Megan vom Fugerhof is owned by Giuseppe Pulina in Italy. Int. Ch. Tina vom Fugerhof also lives in Italy with Roberto Ferraro.

There were three Champions entered at the Austrian show bred by Maria Kaiser of the Kaiserhaus kennels, who also breeds Bernese Mountain Dogs. They were: Ch. Jupiter aus dem Kaiserhaus, owned by Max and Christine Heidi of the Steinfelden kennels, Int. Ch. Kora aus dem Kaiserhaus, owned by Edith Hoblinger of the Hutten Winkel kennels, and Ch. Edgar aus dem Kaiserhaus, owned by Margarete Noppinger. Ch. Kobold vom Rotzenberg represented owner-breeder Heini Kollmer of the Rotzenberg kennels, and other Austrian breeders included Veronika Glawischnig of the Hermannsdorf kennels and Erhard Langer of the Haidmuhle prefix.

HUNGARY AND YUGOSLAVIA

Sandor Kucsora travelled from Hungary to win the Reserve CAC for long-haired dogs at the Austrian WUSB show with Sotetkerti Betyar, bred by Janos Hejas. Bela Siklosi of the St Gallen-Erdei kennels, also of Hungary, had entered Ch. St Gallen-Erdei Exi. Nagypaztai Erik was bred by Tibor Haurancsik and owned by Ildiko Torzsi. Erik's brother, Hungarian Ch. Nagypaztai Eddy, owned by Karoly Imre, was shown at the Italian Club show in 1987. Ch. Odorvari Puma was another Hungarian entrant owned by Zoltan Dallos and bred by Bela Szalontai. There was just one entrant from Yugoslavia. This was Ch. Fil, owned by Boris Simicevic and bred by Stane Vadnov. His father was an English-bred dog, Knockespoch Ambassador.

SCANDINAVIA

DENMARK

Denmark has some of the best St Bernards in Europe. The Hanaethorp kennels of Mr and Mrs de Boer has done exceptionally well at the World Union Shows. Ch. Hanaethorp Rico won Best in Show at Kerkrade in Holland, Ath in Belgium and

Int. Ch. Sankt Cardis Stine.

Vejen in Denmark. His short-haired brother, Ch. Hanaethorp Ruben won Best in Show at the 1991 WUSB show at Saone, France. Rico won the St Bernard trophy outright, as he had won it three years in succession. Ruben is owned by Golveringden of Holland. Mr and Mrs de Boer own another brother, Ch. Hanaethorp Rolf, as well as Ch. Hanaethorp Patrick and Ch. Hanaethorp Ricke.

The Sankt Cardi kennel of Lause and Karen Nielsen is known throughout Europe. Mrs Nielsen regularly attends most major shows in Europe, where she is extremely successful. Some of her Champions include: Ch. Sankt Cardis Evita, Ch. Sankt Cardis Ib, Ch. Sankt Cardis Nimbus, Ch. Sankt Cardis Nelly, Ch. Sankt Cardis Albert, Ch. Sankt Cardis Maximillian, Ch. Sankt Cardis Egil, Ch. Sankt Cardis Stine, Ch. Sankt Cardis Gunter, Ch. Sankt Cardis Kleo, Ch. Sankt Cardis Cardi and Ch. Sankt Cardis Anton. Anton is owned by the best known of the Danish judges, Carl Otto Mastrup, who runs the Kongeaans kennels with his wife Irse.

Some of the other well-known Danish breeders are: Karen Hansen (Sankt Ludwig), Kaj Klysner (Klysner), Simon Lundgaard (Maj), the Jensens (Bisons), Laila Bech (Mosegardens) and Eva Steinberg (Bjornskovs). The Dansk St Bernard Club was founded in 1973, and they held the World Union Show in Vejen over two days – it had previously been confined to a one-day event. Some members of the

Int. Ch. & Dan. Ch. Hanaethorp Ruben winning at the WUSB Show in 1990. Owned by Hans Golverdinger.

Danish club also train their dogs to do Agility as well as Obedience.

NORWAY AND SWEDEN.

The Norwegian and Swedish Saint scene is dominated by the Bernegardens kennels of Britt Marit Halvorsen, who lives in Sweden close to the Norwegian border. Some thirty of the sixty-four entries at the Norwegian Show in 1991 had the Bernegardens prefix, and sixteen of the others were from Bernegardens stock. Best in Show and best long-haired was Bernegarden's Olympus, who has already won nine challenges, but he cannot be a Champion until he is two years of age. The best long-haired bitch was Nor. Ch. Deinhard's Brown Sugar, bred by Karin Byrevik and owned by Katarina Heiberg. The long-haired bitch challenge was won by Bernegarden's Octopussy, owned by Astrid and Arne Nesse. Another of the nineteen-month-old dogs from this '0' litter, Bernegarden's Omega, owned by Ingela Johansson won the short-haired dog challenge. Best short-haired bitch was won by Bernegardens Petite Fleur, owned by her breeder in partnership with Joy Harvey (from New Zealand). Jim Harvey co-owns Olympus with Britt Marit. However, best short-haired in show went to Int. Ch. Nor. Sw. Ch. Athenegardens Charming Apollon, owned by Ole Johannes and Sissel Sorbo, who bred the dog in their Athenegardens kennels.

The Bernegardens kennels have produced over sixty Champions in eleven years. Sw. Nor. Int. Ch. Bernegardens Gulliver and Int. Ch. Nor. Sw. Ch. Bernegardens All Alone are amongst their best known winners. Britt has imported many dogs from the U.S.A., and she also imported Swindridge Florence in whelp to Bernmont Ugglibug in January 1991. Several of the puppies have been successful in the show ring. Other well known kennels in Norway are Ciceronens of Ethna Svendsen Grimstad, St Daniels of Birgitte and Tor E. Danielson, St Moonlights of Kari Denis and St Woods of Katarina Heiberg. The Deinhards kennel of Karin Byrevik bred the Spanish Best in Show winner, Deinhards Madison Avenue. Both the Deinhards and Tootsie Rouls kennels come from Sweden and both have also imported stock from America. Bernegardens stock has been exported to many countries.

FINLAND

The well-known English judge Percy Whittaker has commented on the quality of St Bernards in Finland. We saw Matsaint X1X1, bred by the Mat-Saint kennels in Finland, and owned by Irja Mannisto and Tarja Pahlo. She was of excellent quality and won the Open bitch class at the WUSB show in Denmark. The owners had had to get special permission to take her to the show because of Finland's quarantine regulations.

SOUTH AFRICA

A number of English-bred dogs were exported to South Africa in the seventies and eighties, and these were mainly from the Cornagarth, Lindenhall, Snowranger and Alpentire kennels. The best-known South African breeders of this time were: Hans Steinen of the Arlita kennels, currently chairman of the St Bernard Club of the Transvaal, where there is the greatest concentration of interest in the breed; Mr M. Green of the Dinton kennels was from the same area; Mr Robert Blake of the Crowhill prefix in Cape Town imported stock from Clare Bradley's Snowranger kennels; Mrs Heather Zipp of the Oriel kennels and Mrs Dunlop also from Cape Town, and Mrs D. Cartwright bred St Bernards in Natal.

Ann and Pat went to South Africa in 1986 when Pat was invited to judge the St Bernard Club of Transvaal Championship Show. The club was founded in 1976. The stock at the show was descended from German and Swiss dogs, as well as from English stock. We thought that many of the exhibitors seemed to stick to their own type, rather than mixing them, which one felt could have been to their advantage. From those early breed enthusiasts only Hans Steinen and Mrs Dunlop have remained active in the breed. Mr Steinen had nine dogs who all lived happily together in the house – most of the South African houses are much larger than European homes! He won the bitch CC with Arlita Lucy, out of Ch. Arlita Basko, and also the veteran dog class with a St Bernard of English breeding sired by Ch. Rolf of Cornagarth and Oriel out of Ch. Snowranger Lucerne of Crowhill, bred by Robert Blake.

We were pleased to meet Dieter and Rita Nagel of the Alpenheim kennels. We had just acquired Alpenheim Ernest; he had been brought by his owners to the UK, who had then found they could no longer keep him. He was sired by Ch. Barry vom Hausberg of Alpenheim out of Vera von der Graftschaft Hadamar – both German-bred parents had been imported to South Africa by the Nagels. They have also imported progeny from Int. Ch. Ashbjorn v d Enchial. The late Mr J. Treger showed excellent Swiss-bred stock from Eduard Rodel's Sauliamt kennels, using Sauliamt S.A. as his prefix. Mr and Mrs Horst Kranz based their kennels on the Sauliamt S.A. stock, and bred dogs with the Richtavier prefix. One of their best dogs is Ch. Richtavier Amasco. Sauliamnt S.A. stock was also used in Mr Ghavalas's kennel along with Thorberg lines. He owned Ch. Thorberg Anesta, bred by Mr and Mrs Maurhofer. Ch. Thorberg Peter was the top winner at the time. Mr and Mrs Schraner, owners of the Altburg kennels, were placed at the Swiss Centenary Show with Ch. Alpenheim Conrad of Altberg. His litter brother was Ch. Alpenheim Carlo of

Halcea, owned by Mr J. D. Jensen. Conrad sired Altburg Arnie, owned by Mr and Mrs Labuschagne, a dog of excellent quality. Salburg Adam, bred by Jannie and Wesley Gibbard, has recently been one of the top winners. Mrs Dunlop was showing the Scottish-bred dog Ch. Alpentire Monarch of Alpentire. Other well-known kennels include Tijuana owned by Mrs T. Kirby, Toujours owned by Mrs C. A. Kriger, Vonpeiser owned by Mr and Mrs De la Guerra, the Evergreen kennels owned by Miss C. A. Ebbs, and the Butshor kennels owned by Mr and Mrs Short.

The St Bernard Club of the Transvaal had an extremely enthusiastic Carting section. The dogs have to be trained in basic obedience before they take on this task. Some owners also test the great strength of a St Bernard, and Mr Horst Kranz had a dog that could pull a Volkswagen van on the flat, as well as perform carting duties. The St Bernard following in South Africa is small but enthusiastic, and we have been told that the King of the Zulus has developed an interest in the breed, buying two St Bernard puppies!

AUSTRALIA

St Bernards were known in Australia as long ago as 1880. Walter Beilby states in his *The Dog in Australasia*, published in 1897, that Captain Clark imported Saints in 1880, but they failed to establish themselves. One named early import was Maplecroft Belle, who died without leaving any stock. Beilby records that the first person to introduce and exhibit St Bernards in Australia was Mr E. F. Stephen of Sydney, who owned Monarque III (by Turk out of Ethel), and the well-known Minerva (by Mount Joux out of Beautiful Mona), who went on to win many prizes for Mr Anderson of Kew, Victoria. However, there are records of the Royal Easter Show in New South Wales and listed in the Non Sporting Class is the St Bernard Rough Coat: Dogs or sluts (as bitches were called in those days) seven entries. These included:

Richardson, John J., Survey Department, Sydney: Countess (slut) 3½ years, 28 inches, 108 pounds; by Faust out of Nun.

Wilkinson, August J., Bond Street, Sydney: Brenda (slut) 15 months, 25 inches, 90 pounds; by Alp out of Queen Bess.

The 1886-1887 N.S.W. Show records that Minerva was one of two imported dogs that were shown; the other was Wallace, aged three years and four months, weighing eight stone, and owned by J. Harding of the Bulletin Office, Sydney. Beilby states that "very little advancement was observed from 1883-1887, when a decided move was made. The following year 19 entries were recorded at the Melbourne show, the largest yet by far exhibited in Australia. Mr J. C. Anderson, Capt. J. R. Clark, Messrs T. Liley, P. J. Russell, L. D. Bordsdorff and Miss B. Slade were the chief prize takers."

At this show there were two new imports – Rhoderick Dhu and St Leonards. Rhoderick Dhu was imported by Mr J. C. Anderson, along with Silver Princess, who was in whelp to Dhu. Unfortunately, she died in quarantine. Dhu was already the sire of Don Carlos and Mr W. S. Smith's bitch, Hepsy, who won many prizes in England in 1891 before being sold to America, where she was equally successful. Rhoderick Dhu was a descendant of the original Barry, and was a brindle-patched dog. He was sold to Mr C. Ridley, and did not produce particularly good stock, although he proved to be a foundation line from which several good dogs came. St Leonards was black-and-white, with more white than black. His maternal grandsire was Leonard, who had won the 100 guineas Challenge Cup at the Crystal Palace. He was imported by Mr C. Edgecombe of Adelaide and later sold to Mr Ridley of Victoria. The best of his stock was Mr E. Lock's Kanya Lord Surrey, who was favoured with fashionable markings and was unbeaten among the colonial-bred dogs. Mr Edgecombe had a litter from Kanya Lord Surrey out of his imported bitch, Enid. She was by Sir Henry, a son of Save and Bessie II, who was the dam of Plinlimmon. Jumbo XI was one of the resulting litter, and, apparently lacking in head properties, he was sold in 1891 to Mr J. Sykes of Tasmania. He did well at shows with his new owner, and produced some good stock from the Mynda Lion bitch, including Lady Chester. Another member of the Kanya Lord Surrey litter was Leonas, owned by Mr A. Harris of South Australia. This dog was said to be infinitely superior to his brother in every respect, excepting height. He resembled his sire in markings, but he had more bone, he was heavier and a better mover.

In 1891 Captain Clark imported Baron of Greystoke, a son of Pouf and Lady Onslow. Baron died shortly after his release from quarantine, but he had been visited by a few bitches. The best of his stock was Mrs Abercrombie's Nervelstone Patch, described as a very fine animal indeed, excelling in legs and feet. She died soon after whelping, along with most of the puppies. Lady Lucia was another of Baron's daughters, and it was said that these two were the best pair of colonial-bred bitches. Sir Edwin Smith of Adelaide bought Fairfax, who was the winner of a strong class of puppies at the Kennel Club Show at Olympia in 1889, and his buyer claimed him at his catalogue price of £150. He held an unbeaten record in Australia, besides winning at Melbourne in 1891 and 1892. He was kept mainly as a pet, but he did sire a few offspring. Fairfax was a grandson of Plinlimmon and travelled with a ship-mate, Sweetheart. She was another unfortunate bitch to die with all her puppies – whelping did seem to be very hazardous at this time. Captain Clark next took out the English show winner, Capstan, who lived to quite a good age, and had a successful career in the colonies. He was described as a great favourite at shows, often collecting for charity. He seemed to fare better than most – an alarming number of dogs died en route to Australia, in quarantine, or just after their release; they had all had to cross the equator and the heat must have taken its toll. Mr W. T. Lance of Newcastle, New South Wales, imported the well-known Geraint, a son of Sir Bedivere. Geraint was said to have become sterile – rumours had been very uncomplimentary, even in his early days. The result was that he was bought for £1590 and sold for £200 when still in his prime as a show dog. He did, however, sire a litter to Mr Grosby's imported bitch Peggy II, a granddaughter of Plinlimmon. Several of the New South Wales winners came from this pair, including Newington Nelson, Newington Pilgrim and Sydenham Lion.

The main importers of this era were Mr C. Ridley, who imported several Saints, and Captain Clark. Descendants from the best dogs in England included Save, Sir Bedivere, Plinlimmon, Alp, Cadwallader (Mr Ridley imported Norelia, his granddaughter), and Tell – Mr Lanaley's Wirriwalla Lord is a direct descendant. In New South Wales in 1890 there were ten entries at the Royal Easter Show, which included two short-haired Saints, a few from New Zealand and one from the Hospice. There were forty-one entries in 1896 – the first year that there was official registration. In 1899 entries had dropped to thirty, with a few from Victorian breeders, and by 1900 the entry was down to seventeen, with five of those exhibited from Johan P. Claesson's Sunlight kennels. In 1902 there were nineteen entries, including representatives from Claesson, F. Lansley, H. Johnson, Mr Tremnier and Mr Dalwood. In 1903 there were only eleven, declining to six the following year, and dominated by Mrs Claesson's Champions, including Ch. Sunlight Snow Queen. Mrs Claesson went on to win the Championship three years in succession: in 1906, 1907, and 1908, the last two years with Ch. Woolwich King. The decline in entries resulted in the loss of individual classification, and St Bernards had to be shown in classes for dogs of 45lbs or over. In 1935 there were four entrants, mainly locally bred, but there was also some imported stock. In 1940 entries were down to four dogs and no bitches. The dog Challenge was won by Rothwell St Gothard, owned by A. L. Norman and bred by O. E. Elliot. The dog was sired by Alpine Crusader out of Hospice Lady Eloise. The prize money was: 1st 15 shillings, 2nd 5 shillings, and 3rd 2 1/2 shillings. By 1950 the entry had increased by one, but this time no dog Challenge was awarded. The Challenge bitch went to Blue Mountain Princess Prim owned by Mrs N. Soux and bred by A. E. Wicket. The bitch was sired by Mountain Prince out of Mountain Mistress and whelped in February 1945.

The sixties saw the beginning of a surge of imports from Britain. Mr Kennedy of

Sydney bought Cornagarth Gareth (born 2.10.1960) by Ch. Cornagarth Monbardon Sir Marcus out of Ch. Cornagarth Delilah of Durrowabbey. However, it was Mr Mullane of Sydney who was the main breeder at this time. He bought two imports from the U.K. – Cornagarth Bonnie (born 5.4.1964), bred by A. K. Gaunt, sired by Ch. Cornagarth Democratic out of Ch. Cornagarth Moira, and Fernebrandon New Year's Wish (born 1.1.1963), bred by Dr Una Westell, sired by Ch. Fernebrandon Agrippa and Fernebrandon Corvette. Mr Mullane, of the Mummamia prefix, bred forty-five puppies from six litters, all out of New Year's Wish. The sires were Mummamia Shannandoah, Cornagarth Bonnie and Mummamia Mr Scotland, and two of the progeny, Mummamia Patrick and Mummamia Peter Pan, were exported to Hawaii. Dorothy and Gwen Chisman of New South Wales imported St Rae of Dale End in 1964, St Francis of Dale End in 1968 and Aust. Ch. Vanessa of Dale End in 1969, and all three won many prizes in Australia. Dale End was the prefix of Mrs Read Pearson, a small breeder from the South of England. The Chismans subsequently adopted the name Dale End for their Australian kennels. In 1975 the Australian Dale End kennels bought Cornagarth Chiquita, winner of two CCs in the U.K., in whelp to Ch. Burtonswood Bossy Boots. The litter produced two Champions and her second litter produced five Champions. Some of the home-bred Dale End Champions were: Ch. Dale End St Ramon, Ch. Dale End St Angella, the brother and sister Ch. Dale End St Nicholas and Ch. Dale End St Moira, who won the Dog and Bitch Challenge at the Sydney Royal and Spring Fair; and Ch. Dale End St Anthony – the Victorian Kennel Club Dog of the year in 1980.

Australian Ch. Karl of Cornagarth was imported by Mrs L. Briggs (Snowsaint) in 1972. He was bred by Mr Michael Braysher out of Cornagarth Kuno v Birkenkopf (German) and Ch. Burtonswood Big Time, and he carried the Cornagarth prefix of A. K. Gaunt, who exported him. He was the sire of approximately seventeen Champions and appears in many pedigrees today. He was the sire of the first St Bernard litter reared in Victoria for many years – the dam was Ch. Mummamia Andrea.

Mrs Sandra Ormsby was secretary of the St Bernard Club in New South Wales, founded in 1976, until her death in 1984. Mr and Mrs Ormsby owned the Paxis kennels, and one of their best dogs was Ch. Daneeal Targus, bred by Mrs I. Laurence of Sydney. He was sired by Ch. Karl of Cornagarth out of a U.S.A. import, Karacsonya Dee Dee of Pal Mal, and he won many CCs and awards, including Best in Show at the St Bernard Club Show in 1980. One of his daughters, Ch. Zebedee Alpine Melody, owned by Paxis, was bred to the German import Aramis von der Kurstadt, and produced Ch. Paxis Amos. The Merribuff kennels of Mesdames Dowsey and Bridges is one of the best known kennels in Victoria. They imported Aust. Ch. Whaplode Great Expectations from the Harphams and they have bred some of the best St Bernards in Australia. The 1980 St Bernard of the Year (N.S.W.) was Aust. Ch. Ragdale Santa Claus, owned by the Devawn Kennels of Dave and Eve Acton. Santa Claus was the son of Aust. Ch. Benem Sir Arthur of Whaplode and Snowranger Noelle, both imported from England. The Freesia prefix is another well known prefix from N.S. W., owned by Gwen Hughes.

The St Bernard Club of Victoria was started in 1975, and the president is Mrs Ivy Wallace of the Allsaints kennels. Mrs Nikki Chapman returned to Australia from England and took with her Aust. Ch. Illustrious of Burtonswood and Fitzwilly. She founded the St Bernard Club of Southern Australia in 1981. Ch.Devonmist Montgomery is another well known Saint from South Australia. Queensland had an interesting import with Glasslyn Rocket, who came from Eire. The Bernebrook kennels, owned by Shia and Vic Palmer, who also breed Mastiffs, and the Arym kennels are also active on the St Bernard front. Other imports who have been the foundation of today's stock include Alpentire Clara Bow, who went out in whelp to Ch. Lindenhall Capability Brown; Lindenhall The Joker, Whaplode My Girl, Aust. Ch. Grand Lad of Cornagarth and My Lady Emma, the dam of the Benem litter born in Britain. Big Ben v Schwarzaaldhof was an import from the U.S.A. Many of these names will by now have vanished from the back of the pedigrees, but they are the ancestry of today's Australian St Bernards.

TASMANIA

The St Bernard Social Club of Tasmania was founded in 1981 by a few enthusiasts. It has less than a hundred members today, but they are very active and the club publishes a magazine to keep everyone in touch with what is going on.

John, Judy and their daughter Susan Tenniswood own the Boroniahill kennels at Kingston Beach, Tasmania. We first met them some ten years ago when they were on holiday in England and Scotland, and they later accompanied us on a trip to Holland to see a Dutch show. Their most famous dog was Aust. Ch. Tremel Distant Saint. He was imported from the Tremel St Bernards of Stan, Rhona and Steven Haywood in Cornwall, England. He was Best in Show at the Royal Hobart Show in 1985, top St Bernard for three years in 1984, 1985 and 1986, and he was runner-up dog for three years in 1987, 1988 and 1989. He accumulated over 1000 Challenge points. Ch. Tremel Faraway Lady went out to Tasmania with Distant Saint to the Actongold kennels of Des and Madge Burn. This bitch was also extremely successful in the show ring. Sue and Allan Johnson of the Lympne kennels bred Ch. Lympne Mistress Debbie in 1979 from the U.K. imports Heidan Black Prince and Maurbry Minnie Anna, who were both short-haired. Maurbry Mitsey Ann, Minnie's

Aust. Ch. Tremel Distant Saint. Owned by John and Judy Tenniswood.

sister, another short-haired Saint, also made the trip. Aust. Ch. Whaplode My Explorer became a top stud for the Lympne kennels, and they subsequently bought Whaplode My Quartermaster. Whaplode My Pollyanna was owned by the Sayers. The Lympne Saints are still a very successful kennel, and the kennel has now moved to Queensland. The Noblesaint kennels, owned by Karen Vout has been operating in Tasmania for over ten years. She was showing Ch. Lontana Park Abacus back in 1981, and was competing in obedience with Merribuff Bernadina CD, as well as in the show ring.

NEW ZEALAND

The quarantine laws of all the Australian states and Australasian countries stated that dogs could only be imported from the U.K. If they came from any other country they had to have six months quarantine, followed by a further six months in the U.K., and even then they were subjected to a further period of quarantine on arrival. This meant that nearly all the imports came from Britain, as the cost of importing from any other country was astronomical. New Zealand imported many Saints in the seventies, mainly from the Jonjersi kennels of the late Audrey French, Cornagarth, Snowranger of Bradley and Hill, Burtonswood (M. Hindes) and Mrs M. Chapman's

Maurbry kennels. These included N.Z. Ch. Jonjersi Toynbee by Snowranger Lohengrin out of Monterosa St Delilah. He sired thirty-six puppies, and many became Champions. He was owned by Mr and Mrs Harbeck of Christchurch. N.Z. Ch. Jonjersi St Royale was by Snowranger Jaunty, a son of the Dutch import to the U.K., Ch. Snowranger Bas v d Vrouenpolder, out of Snowranger Angelique, a daughter of Snowranger Tello v Sauliamt. She was imported by Helene Steele of Kaiapoi. This bitch had three litters – sixteen puppies in total – sired by the U.K. import N.Z. Ch. Ingfield Benedict, bred by Silvia Johnson out of Lindenhall High Authority and Snowranger Lucretia. Five of the puppies went to Australia. The Steeles are breeders of the well known Eleets kennels. N.Z. Ch. Maurbry Maily was imported by Mr L. G. Thurston of Rotorua in 1976. This dog was by Maurbry Marquinn out of Benem Lady Be Good. He was said to have been unbeaten in the show ring, and was one of the very few Saints to be H.D. free. Maurbry Most Southern Star was another import from the Maurbry kennels. Other imports of the seventies included N.Z. Ch. Burtonswood Famous Boots and N.Z. Ch. Katie Kakebaker of Gerunda. The Tai Yuan kennels owned by C. A. Rogers and C. M. Tippett have made an outstanding contribution, and they have made up some twenty-one Champions. They were also successful in artificially inseminating their N.Z. Ch. Tai Yuan Claudia with sperm from Ch. Whaplode My Lord in 1984. Coatham Sporting Chance and Leo The Lionheart of Coatham were exported from the Coatham kennels of Maureen and George Gwilliam in the eighties.

Recently, dogs have been imported to New Zealand from Scandinavia, which, like Britain is rabies-free. Jim and Joy Harvey of the Bernedale kennels imported N.Z. Ch. Bernegardens Lachelis from Brit Marit Halvorsen in Sweden. He was sired by Nor. Sw. & Int. Ch. Bernegardens All Alone out of Nor. Ch. Dein Hards Winona. They also imported Bernegardens Yerba by Nor. Sw. and Int. Ch. Bernegardens Gulliver and Nor. Sw. and Finnish Ch. Bernegardens Moonbeam. They own N.Z. Ch. Bernegardens Joker Adamson in partnership with the Chablais kennels. He is sired by All Alone out of Nor. Sw. Ch. Betzebas Asheeba Ann. Malcolm S. Simons of the Chenalette kennels owns Bernegardens Golden Poppy, and Mary Gill has Bernegardens Elvira Madegan. The well known N.Z. Aust. Ch. Sedna I'm Sigrid was owned by the D'Mowbray kennels of J. Mowbray and P. Groves, formerly of New South Wales. The Bernabby kennels of P. Potter and A. Laird also have several Champions. The San Bernardino kennels, owned by V. & A. Rogers, Staglands owned by C. A. Simister, Xzon owned by Roy Down, Chamonix owned by the Cochrans, Zollikofen owned by the Simpsons, and Anahera owned by Stevenson and Sharp are all actively involved in the breed at the current time.

Chapter Nine

IN THE SHOW RING

If you intend to show your St Bernard, the first step is to contact a breed club. There are numerous St Bernard Clubs in America, often several to one state, so it would be advisable to ask the American Kennel Club for a list. In Europe each country usually has one national breed club, sometimes with regional branches, and the secretary's address can be obtained from the national Kennel Club. In Britain, the principal breed clubs are the English St Bernard Club and the St Bernard Club of Scotland. There is also the United St Bernard Club, and two other regional clubs: the Eastern St Bernard Club and the South of England St Bernard Club. When you have made contact with a breed club, find out the date of their Club Show or Specialty Show: this will give you the opportunity of seeing many more St Bernards in the show ring than if you go to a general Championship or All Breeds Show. The leading breeders will either be exhibiting or managing the show, and so you can watch how St Bernards are shown, and pick up some useful advice.

It is a good idea to attend ringcraft classes before competing in your first show. This will enable both you and your dog to learn what is required. Before arriving at the show your dog must be clean, preferably bathed, and well groomed. General appearance goes a long way, and a clean well-behaved dog will stand a far better chance of winning than a scruffy badly-trained one. There are plenty of good dog shampoos available, but remember that chalk and white powders in the coat are contrary to Kennel Club rules, and should not be used.

In the United Kingdom, entries for shows can close up to two months in advance, and so you must make your plans well ahead. In other countries there is more flexibility, as entries remain open until nearer the date of the show. Classification in Britain is usually: Puppy 6-12 months (a few shows put on Minor Puppy 6-9 months), Junior 6-18 months, possibly Special Yearlings 6-24 months; and then some classes are scheduled for Maiden, Novice, Undergraduate, Graduate, Postgraduate, Minor Limit, Mid-limit and Limit, which go according to the number of first prizes the dog has won. The definitions of classes can be found in the show schedule, and all shows put on an Open class which, as its name implies, is open to all. Champions in Britain are shown in the Open class. To become a Champion, a dog must win three Challenge Certificates under three different judges. CCs are on offer at Championship Shows for the Best Dog and the Best Bitch, providing that the judge thinks that they are of such outstanding merit as to be worthy of the title of 'Champion'. A judge can withhold the CC if he or she wishes to do so. In order to be awarded Junior Warrant, a dog must get 25 points between the age of 12 and 18 months. These are allocated as follows: 3 points for a first prize in a breed class at a Championship Show, and 1 point for a first prize at an Open Show.

In the U.S.A. classification is usually: 6-9 months, 9-12 months, 12-18 months, Novice, Bred by Exhibitor, American Bred, Open Long-Haired, Open Short-Haired, Veteran, Stud Dogs and Brood Bitches. Champions compete for Best of Breed only. Points differ according to the State, and are allocated according to the number of exhibits present. The number of points available will be printed in the schedule, which is known as the Premium List. The points towards gaining a Championship are awarded to the Winners Dog and Winners Bitch, based on the actual number of dogs present. If the Winners Dog or Winners Bitch is also awarded Best of Breed, the number of dogs of both sexes and those competing for Best of Breed are added together when calculating the Championship points. If the dog designated Winners Dog or Winners Bitch is also awarded Best of Opposite Sex to Best of Breed, the dogs of its own sex that have been defeated for Best of Opposite Sex are counted, in addition to the dogs that competed in the regular classes. The dog awarded Best of Winners is credited with whichever is the greater of the points awarded to the Winners Dog or the Winners Bitch. To obtain the title of Champion, a dog must win 15 points: 6 or more must have been won at two shows with a rating of 3 or more Championship points each, and under two different judges; the remaining balance must be won under a third judge.

Southern Ireland has a similar points system to the U.S.A., and among the total accumulated there must be at least one five point Green Star. The rest of Europe has a similar system to the English. In most of these countries a dog needs four C.A.C.'s to gain the title of National Champion. Some of the larger shows have C.A.C.I.B.'s on offer, and to become an International Champion a dog must win four C.A.C.I.B.'s in three different countries. The classes are either age-based or Open, but the majority of Europe puts on separate classes for long-haired and short-haired St Bernards, each with their own separate C.A.C.'s.

It is not wise to enter a young puppy in anything other than its own age class; it will look completely out of place with more mature dogs. Youngsters just over twelve months can be entered in the 'lower' classes, and the points go towards the Junior Warrant. In Europe it is usual to handle your own dog, but in the U.S.A. professional handlers are often employed – sometimes the dog lives with the handler and travels to shows with him. There are often three or four shows over several days, and the handler often takes several dogs belonging to different owners and from different breeds to show on each day. In England professional handlers are rarely used other than for the Terrier breeds.

In preparation for the show, you should pack a show bag. This should include:

Grooming brushes.
Grooming comb.
Scissors.
Towels – to mop up the drool and for a last minute rub-down.
An aerosol dry shampoo – these are usually spirit-based, and we use them to give our dogs a final clean-up before they go into the ring. Unfortunately, white powders and chalk are no longer permitted in Britain. There are spray whiteners, which are allowed, but they need to be rubbed out of the coat before the dog enters the ring.
A bib – this will help to keep the dog's chest clean while it is waiting on the bench; it can get very wet and dirty from salivating.
A tub of Vaseline or a bottle of baby oil – both products are equally good, and we regard them as a necessity. The oil or Vaseline should be rubbed on the nose, and it is surprising how this brightens the black colour, making the dog look as though it glows with health.
A plastic lemon containing lemon juice – this is a useful item of first aid medication in hot weather. If the dog's breathing is laboured because it is over-heated, a squirt of lemon will help to clear the throat of saliva and will aid the breathing.
Benching collar and chain – a dog should never be benched on a choke chain as it could jump off the bench and literally hang itself.
A show lead – we always use these in the ring, but if you are handling a large or difficult dog, you may need a choke chain.
A bench-rug or blanket – this is not essential, but your dog will appreciate the extra comfort when it is lying on the bench.

A water bowl or bucket.

A plastic bottle of water – water is available at all shows, but the dog may need a drink en route.

A poop-scoop, plastic bag or suitable container to collect your dog's excrement – fouling of public places is not permitted.

The St Bernard is not usually baited in the ring, so there is no need to bring titbits. However, if you are travelling a long distance to a show you may need to take the dog's dinner and a dish to feed it. Do not forget the obvious – like show passes and money. One lady once told us that she was going down the motorway when she realised that she had forgotten the most important item of all – the dog!

All major shows are benched, so when you arrive at the show the first thing to do is to find your bench and settle your dog. Then find the ring, and ascertain what time your class is scheduled. Your ring number will either be on your bench, or it will be given to you in the ring by the steward. When judging commences, your class will be called and exhibitors go and stand in a line in the ring. In the U.K., you can stand anywhere you like, on the continent it is more orderly and exhibitors must stand in numerical order. When you stand in line you should pose your dog. You should be holding the lead in your left hand, and the dog should be standing sideways on to the judge. Make sure it is standing squarely with its head up. The judge will often ask the exhibitors to run their dogs round the ring once, and will then assess each dog individually. In the rest of Europe the dogs are usually walked round the ring.

Your dog should be stood squarely for the judge to go over it – make sure that none of its legs are stuck out in an ungainly manner. You will probably be asked your dog's age, but only answer the questions that the judge asks – do not try and enter into a conversation. If the dog is a male, the judge will check to see if it is entire. In some countries this is not necessary, as the dogs are examined by a vet before being allowed into the ring, and if a dog is not entire it would be excluded at this point. The judge will then look into your dog's mouth to see if it has the correct bite and correct dentition. Some judges feel the dogs more than others – though we believe that a competent judge can see most points without over-handling the exhibits.

The next stage is to move your dog. Listen carefully to the instructions you are given; in most instances you will be asked to move straight up and down, and then in a triangle. You may be asked to move your dog slowly or quickly, and it is important that you respond to the instructions, otherwise the judge may think your dog does not move well when it is going at a different pace. On the continent a dog is frequently instructed to move at a walking pace – and this occasionally happens in

Britain and America. In fact, walking shows up a lot of movement faults that are not as visible when the dog is running. After the judge has seen each dog move, exhibitors will be asked to line up again and places will be awarded.

Always be sporting and gracious, whether you win or lose. Of course you will be delighted if your dog wins, but if you are placed down the line, do not tear your prize cards up in a temper, or show obvious disapproval of the decisions that have been made. Unfortunately, this sort of behaviour is seen occasionally, but it is intolerable. You will not make friends in the dog world by being a bad sport. There is always another show, another day. You may go to the judge after the class and ask for an opinion of your dog. There are some bad judges about, and some are biased, but the majority do know what they are doing. You may think that the judge is an idiot, but if you have not been in the dog game long, you could be wrong. After all, beauty is in the eye of the beholder – and while you think that your pet is a world-beater, there could be better dogs around.

Chapter Ten

BREEDING

Breeding St Bernards has never been the easiest of hobbies. Many people decide to breed a litter when they already have a bitch. It is doubtful whether you would be able to buy an adult bitch for breeding, unless you were prepared to pay a lot of money for her. There are very few kennels that would sell a good brood bitch unless they were overstocked, although some may let one go on full or part breeding terms. This usually involves a deal where the kennel gets some of the puppies from the bitch's litter, rather than charging a full price for the sale of the bitch. If you enter into any such arrangement, make sure you have a signed agreement stating the terms of the deal. However friendly you are with the kennel-owner, misunderstandings can occur, and doing business with friends does not always work.

If you are looking for a stud dog to use on your bitch, beware of the breeder who says that he has 'just the dog for your bitch', or the breeder who offers you the use of his dog for nothing – there is bound to be a catch. Perhaps nobody else wants to use the dog, and this could be for very good reasons. If you do not pay a stud fee, the stud dog owner will probably want pick of litter, and so you must decide whether you are prepared to lose your best puppy. Again, make sure you get your agreement in writing. Most breeders are honest, but you should always be aware of the possible pitfalls. There are a minority of breeders who cannot see good in anyone's stock other than their own, and these people are best avoided when you are embarking on your own breeding programme; there are plenty of experienced breeders who will give advice, and perhaps most important of all, they will give an unbiased opinion as to which is the best stud dog to suit your bitch.

All breeds suffer from hereditary problems, and it is important to try to eradicate these, as far as possible, from your breeding programme. Hip dysplasia affects many breeds, and unfortunately a large number of St Bernards suffer from this condition to some degree. Some countries have tried various methods in an attempt to control it. For example, any dog that is imported into Scandinavia has to pass an X-ray test to ensure it is sound enough to be used for breeding. In Germany all dogs must be X-rayed before they are used for breeding, and they are graded into five categories:

0 = Free.
1 = Bordering.
2 = Light.
3 = Average.
4 = Severe.

A total of 1045 St Bernards were evaluated between 1983 and 1986. The results were:

Free	17.5 per cent.
Bordering	14.5 per cent.
Light	17.3 per cent.
Average	31.2 per cent.
Severe	19.5 per cent.

In 1990 129 dogs were evaluated, and the results showed a considerable overall improvement:

Free	28.7 per cent.
Bordering	20.2 per cent.
Light	21.6 per cent.
Average	24.8 per cent.
Severe	4.7 per cent.

These results show the value of a compulsory X-ray system, although bad hind movement cannot be not entirely attributed to hip dysplasia. We have seen dogs with bad rear movement in Germany with a 0 grading. In England the short-haired St Bernard Cornagarth Askan was X-rayed because he had such poor rear movement, and was found to be free of HD. The British system of hip-scoring is not compulsory, and thus its value is open to controversy. The scoring ranges from 0 to

106; scores are given on each side and then both sides are added together to get the overall score.

$$0/0 \quad = \quad \text{HD-free}$$
$$\text{Up to } 8 \quad = \quad \text{Exceptionally good.}$$
$$22 \quad = \quad \text{The breed average.}$$

Any score below 22 is considered good.

The St Bernards that have hip-scores below 8 can be counted on one hand. There are Champions in the breed with scores of up to 30. The Kennel Club recognises the scoring system, but there is no ruling which prohibits breeding with dogs with hip dysplasia, no matter how badly they may suffer from it. This crucial decision is therefore left entirely to the discretion of the breeder. In order to be hip-scored, a dog must be anaesthetised, and as there is always a small element of risk attached to this procedure, many breeders dislike having it done, or they may wait until a dog needs an anaesthetic for another reason. There has been considerable research on hip dysplasia over recent years, and now some authorities claim that only 40 per cent of the cases can be attributed to heredity, with feeding, rearing and environment being the other influential factors. Certainly, lack of muscle in the hindleg often occurs in cases where a dog is suffering from hip dysplasia.

A brood bitch should always be sound and of reasonable type. It is not always the best bitches in the show ring which make the best broods. In fact, many of the top bitches in England have been useless for reproduction. Perhaps they have suffered too much stress during their show career, or possibly they pick up some infection as a result of travelling from show to show – the reason for this failure in breeding has not been ascertained. This problem is not confined to St Bernards: it is noticeable that the top-winning bitches in other breeds rarely go on to be good producers. Some St Bernard breeders choose an exceptionally large bitch for breeding, in order to cement this desirable quality in their stock. However, this can be disastrous, as, in our experience, these bitches often fail to conceive. We have often wondered whether this could be because bitches of this type carry too many male hormones. The use of steroids can also cause sterility.

A bitch that has any glaring faults, such as a badly undershot jaw or extremely light eyes, should not be used for breeding. A mis-marked bitch, of good conformation and type, may occasionally be used to preserve a line. However, this should only be undertaken by an experienced breeder who is fully conversant with the background of the dogs that are being used. We have found that it is often the smaller bitch that makes the best brood. Study your bitch's pedigree, and then

Ch. Swindridge Catherine: an outstanding brood bitch – all the Swindridge Champions can be traced back to her   *A. Roslin Williams*

examine the pedigree of any stud dog that you may want to use. If you are a novice, it is tempting to put your trust in the stud dog owner when it comes to selecting a suitable mate for your bitch. This is fine if you are dealing with a breeder of discretion, who knows the lines and background of his dogs, and if there are several dogs to choose from. Never use the dog that is located nearest to you, just for the sake of convenience. If you are embarking on breeding a litter, it is an expensive business, and it is vital that you start off by choosing the dog that will complement your bitch. You must decide whether you want to use a long-haired or a short-haired sire. In Germany, it is customary to mate a long-haired to a short-haired. In Britain and the U.S.A. the short-haired, or smooth variety, is not nearly as popular as the long-haired, and few breeders would mate two short-haired Saints together. We did this many years ago, and the result was nine short-haired and one long-haired. In Britain, the long-haired, or rough variety, are predominantly rough-bred, and two roughs mated together (of English ancestry) will always produce roughs. If long-haired and short-haired are crossed, the result will generally be some of each variety. The crossing of a curly or open-coated rough to a short-haired will improve the

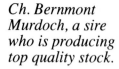

*Ch. Bernmont
Murdoch, a sire
who is producing
top quality stock.*

density of the coats of the rough or long-haired progeny. However, short-haired puppies do not always sell as readily as long-haired, and this is an important consideration for all breeders.

If you wish to line breed, that is, breed to an exceptional dog or bitch in your bitch's line, be careful to find out whether there are any weaknesses in your bitch's pedigree, or you stand the risk of magnifying any problems. If your bitch is already line bred or in-bred, it might be wise to use a complete outcross, or at least choose a dog that has one side of its pedigree unrelated to the bitch's line. When the breed was in-bred in the fifties and sixties, it got to the stage where many of the Champions were unsound. Breeding type to type usually gets the best results, although you usually have to wait a generation before getting top class stock from a completely different type, such as an import. The import Kuno von Birkenkopf sired a lot of excellent stock in the first generation, although he was used a great deal. However, the imports Marshall van Zwing Uri, King von St Klara Kloster and Pankraz von den drei Helmen produced the odd Champion in the first generation, but in the second generation they produced a lot more top quality stock.

When you have selected a stud dog, you should advise the stud dog's owner as soon as your bitch comes into season. The signs to look for are a swelling of the vulva and a bloody discharge. The bitch will usually stand for the dog around ten to twelve days into the season. You can usually tell whether she is ready for mating by

Ch. Pankraz von den Drei Helmen of Bernmont produced his best stock in the second generation.

touching her back end, and she will respond by twisting her tail to one side and standing firm. Often, a good stud dog will not show any interest in the bitch until she is ready for mating. In our opinion, many bitches miss, i.e. fail to conceive, because they are mated too late on in their season. The dog's sperm remains active in the bitch for forty-eight hours, and a mating a little early is far better than leaving it too late. There is no need to wait for the discharge to cease before mating, although it may be changing from a red colour to pink before she is ready. Some bitches that fail to become pregnant may need mating at an unusual time. We had a bitch who we could not get in whelp, and then when she was five years old, we mated her on the first day of her season and she had eight puppies! Some bitches that fail to conceive may have some infection which can be treated with antibiotics. A vet can also give a lutenising hormone, which will make a bitch ovulate, and it may also help infertility.

THE MATING

Some bitches are quite easy to mate, others can be extremely difficult. The usual method of holding the bitch is for the bitch's owner to hold her at the front end. She should be wearing a collar, rather than a choke chain. A good stud dog will mount a bitch and mate her immediately; some like to lick the bitch's ears and wash her face, as part of the courtship. If the dog fails to show any interest in the bitch she may pounce at him and push her rear at him, trying to tantalise him into some action. It is usually necessary for the newcomer to seek the assistance of an experienced breeder to mate a St Bernard. Some will mate on their own with no human assistance, but these are in the minority, and a dog left with a bitch will often wear himself out getting nowhere.

The stud dog owner will usually hold the bitch over his or her knee, and assist the dog to enter the bitch. It is helpful if there is a third person to hold the dog. Some breeders favour using a breeding rack to hold the bitch. This can prevent the person who has their knee under the bitch from getting a badly bruised leg, which can happen when the dog is on the bitch's back. When the dog mounts the bitch he needs to get his front end well over her back, in order to get near enough to her. Some dogs will fool around and mount the wrong end, but the bitch will usually growl and snap if this happens. If you are mating a particularly big bitch to a smaller dog, a raised board can be used. This should be placed immediately behind the bitch's back legs to give the dog extra height. If the bitch is snapping and growling at the dog, put a muzzle on her so that she cannot bite him, and you will not get caught up in the cross-fire.

When the dog mates the bitch his penis enlarges, and a knot forms at the rear after he has entered the bitch's vulva to lock inside her. This prevents the sperm from escaping, and it is known as the tie. If the knot comes up before the dog has entered the bitch, he needs holding back until it has gone down before he has another attempt. When the dog is tied to the bitch, he will drop his front feet down off the bitch and bring one back leg over, so that he is standing back to back with her. The tie usually lasts for ten to twenty minutes, and a mating is seldom successful unless there is a good tie. Most breeders are trustworthy, but to be on the safe side, you should feel that the dog is tied to the bitch. The tie lasts until the knot goes down and they separate. It is important that the dog and bitch stand quietly during this time. If the mating is unassisted, common sense seems to prevail, the dog and bitch do not pull each other around – possibly because the bitch has to be completely receptive to the dog for a natural mating to occur. However, in an assisted mating, where the partners may not be so cooperative, they should be held during the tie. If they do try to break apart it is essential to hold them, so that they do not hurt each other.

THE PREGNANCY

The first sign that a bitch is in whelp is an enlargement of the nipples, and a slight puffiness in this area about three weeks after the mating. Most vets say this is the best time to feel whether a bitch is pregnant, although with a bitch that is as big and solid as a St Bernard, this is not always possible. The present-day method of scanning can detect if a bitch is pregnant from four weeks onwards, although it is not very accurate when it comes to predicting the size of the litter. We have heard of wide discrepancies between the number of foetuses that showed up on the scan, and the number of puppies actually born.

The bitch should have been in good health when she was mated, and so she should not need any extra vitamins or calcium supplements until she is about five weeks in whelp. She should have been wormed prior to mating and when she is four weeks in whelp. By the time she is five to six weeks in whelp, she should be fed twice a day. If you feed a complete food, use the higher protein variety that is recommended for breeding bitches. It should not be necessary to add supplements to these high-quality complete feeds. However, if you feed meat and biscuit, you will need to add extra vitamins and calcium to the bitch's rations.

Suitable accommodation should be prepared for the bitch well in advance. A whelping box should be constructed, and this should be made of material that is easy to clean. We have found that a lining of non-slip linoleum or some other type of vinyl floor covering works very well. The ideal measurements for the whelping box are 6ft. by 5ft. (approximately 180cms. by 150cms.) The sides should be about 1ft. (30cms.) tall, with a 'pig rail' about 6ins. wide (15cm.) jutting out all the way round. The purpose of this is to stop the bitch sitting on the puppies, or trapping them between herself and the side of the box. Alternatively, you can build the rail into a kennel. It is a good idea to have a portion of the kennel for the bitch and her puppies, and a separate portion for the bitch, which she can use when the puppies get a bit older. Some bitches are very good with their puppies, others can be extremely clumsy, and in a breed as big as a St Bernard, this can result in a puppy suffocating under the weight of its mother. The bitch is due to whelp approximately sixty-three days after the mating, but they can be up to three days early or three days late, and still whelp without problems. Occasionally, a bitch can be even later than this and be perfectly alright, but unless you are an experienced breeder, it is wise to seek veterinary advice if the bitch is overdue.

Chapter Eleven

WHELPING

The majority of St Bernards are good, caring mothers, and they rarely experience problems when they are whelping. Before whelping starts, the bitch will produce an abundant clear discharge, which may go green before the first puppy is born. A black discharge is usually the sign of a dead puppy. When a puppy arrives, it should be in a clear bag attached to the placenta, although in many cases the placenta is detached and the bag is broken on delivery. This is no cause for concern; the placenta will come away later. Some bitches will eat the placentas, and this is said to aid the whelping, but others are not interested in doing this. The bag or sac that encloses the puppy must be broken immediately in order to clear its face. The bitch will probably lick the puppy vigorously, but some bitches do not bother to do this. The puppy, which will usually weigh from $1\frac{1}{2}$ to 2 lbs at birth, should be dried with a towel, rubbing facing downwards to clear the lungs. If the puppy appears lifeless, shake it and rub it vigorously – some whelps that have been a long time in birth can be revived. A puppy that is born dead often has very white feet. If the umbilical chord is bleeding, tie it off about one inch from the puppy, with a piece of cotton.

The puppies should be put on to the bitch as soon as they are born. If a puppy is reluctant to suckle, put the puppy's mouth on to the bitch's teat and gently press it to squeeze the teat, and this will give the puppy a taste of the milk. If the bitch is having a large litter, it may be advisable to put the puppies into a box after they have had a feed. Many bitches cannot cope with having all the puppies round them while they are still actually whelping. Other bitches will be upset if you try to remove the puppies, so you will need to assess the situation. The puppies need to be kept warm, and an infra-red lamp hanging over the whelping box is a good form of heat. If it is very cold, you may need two lamps. The whelping box should be lined with newspaper, and this will need to be changed after a delivery, as it will soon become soaked.

The average size of a litter is eight, although we had a bitch that whelped eighteen puppies. Fourteen of these were born alive, and we reared them all, even though we had to help the bitch by supplementing the feeding of the puppies with the bottle. In most cases when a bitch has an exceptionally large litter such as this, the last few are often stillborn, usually through no other cause than the long duration of the whelping. In both Germany and France only six puppies can be registered from any one litter, and culling is more a matter of course than it is in Britain. This is always a difficult issue; the advantages are that only the best specimens survive, and the mother is not put under undue strain, but it is very much a breeder's personal decision. We have found that a very small litter, or a singleton, is often more trouble to rear than a large one. The bitch tends to lick the puppy too much so that it is always wet, and she can literally kill it with kindness.

After the bitch has finished whelping, it is advisable to wash her back end, particularly if she has heavy feathering on her back legs, as she will be soaked in green-coloured fluid. A piece of polyester fur-bedding is the best bedding for the new litter. It is warm for the puppies to lie on, and it also gives them something to grip on as they crawl about. The puppies are born with their eyes closed. They will not open for ten to fourteen days, and at this time they will appear to be darkish-blue in colour. Do not be alarmed: they will change to brown by the time the puppy is six weeks old, although the haw in the corner of the eye will still look blue. This does not go red until the puppy is about eight weeks old; sometimes the haw does not go red, but changes to a brown colour.

If the bitch has not given birth to a puppy within two hours of emitting the green discharge, or if she appears distressed, you must call the vet. She may need an injection to get her going, or she may need a caesarian operation. In our experience, if the bitch is carrying the puppies very low, and she looks as though she has a football hanging in her stomach, she will probably need a caesarian. If this happens, you will need to take the bitch to the vet's surgery. You will also need to take a cardboard box, lined with polyester fur bedding, and a hot-water bottle wrapped in a towel, ready to receive the puppies. If this happens out of normal hours, you must be prepared to assist, in case a veterinary nurse is not available. The vet gets the puppies out very quickly, and he may need help rubbing them dry or reviving them. If a bitch has had a caesarian, do not leave her alone with her puppies until she has completely regained consciousness from the anaesthetic. Equally, if she is a maiden bitch, i.e. one that has never had any puppies before, make sure that she is happy and settled with her new offspring before you leave her. In forty years of breeding St Bernards, we have only had one bitch who would have harmed her puppies, and that was after a caesarian. However, some bitches may take a little while to get used to their puppies; the first sign of acceptance is usually when they start licking them. After a caesarian, the bitch's milk may dry up for a day or two, but it usually returns later. If this happens, you will have to bottle-feed. This can be done with a baby's feeding bottle, and a good quality milk powder made especially for puppies. We recommend Whelpi, but the directions tell you to give a new-born St Bernard one teaspoonful every two hours. We have found this totally inadequate, and we start off with two teaspoonfuls every two hours, increasing it as the puppy appears to need it, but always making sure that the stomach does not feel too distended. If the bitch is not nursing her puppies, you will also have to assist them with passing urine and excreta. You will need some cotton wool, and then you should gently rub the stomach next to the sexual organs to make the puppy pass water, and then rub gently under the tail to make the bowels work. This has to be done after each bottle feed.

The bitch should have plenty of milk by the time she has finished whelping. Some bitches have milk as early as two weeks before the puppies are born, others do not start lactating until after the birth; very occasionally a bitch fails to come into milk. If this should happen, you will have to bottle-feed the litter until they are ready to be weaned. New-born puppies need to be fed day and night, every two hours. By the time they are two weeks old, they should be fed every three hours, with a 'short night', i.e. missing one feed. By this time, you will almost certainly be wondering why you wanted puppies in the first place!

If the bitch appears very restless a couple of days after whelping, it could be the first sign of eclampsia, commonly called milk fever (see Chapter Fourteen), and she will need to be given an injection of calcium solution as quickly as possible If you detect any hard lumps on the teats this can be a sign of mastitis. This will cause problems not only for the bitch, but also for the puppies, as she will be reluctant to feed them, so it is important to call in the vet. The condition can be treated with a course of antibiotics.

Chapter Twelve

FEEDING AND REARING

Most mothers will feed their puppies from birth until weaning age. It is only necessary to hand-feed orphan litters and very large litters, or you may have to help out if the mother has insufficient milk. We have found that a baby's bottle and teat are the easiest to use when you are bottle-feeding puppies. These should be kept in a sterilising solution and rinsed well before each feed. In a normal situation, when the mother is able to care for her puppies herself, the litter should not need any special attention for the first ten days or so, beyond being fed and kept warm – the puppies will usually sleep and feed a good deal of the time. When they are four days old the back dewclaws should be removed. Removal of the front dewclaws is entirely optional, although their removal does give a neater line. Experienced breeders usually do this job themselves. However, anyone else should let the vet do it. Puppies can be wormed from as early as two weeks of age using a paste preparation from the vet. We then repeat the treatment every two weeks using tablets until the puppy is three months of age. The puppies are wormed again at six months, and then two weeks later to clear any eggs. From then onwards we worm our dogs twice a year. The worming preparation should be obtained from a vet, particularly if you are treating young puppies.

The litter will become more active from two to three weeks of age, and this is the time to start teaching them how to lap. Make sure you take the mother away, particularly when the pups are beginning to lap. Some bitches will never take their puppies' food, others have no such scruples! We have found that it is easier to get

Cossethay Lady Elenor of Silversaints with her week-old litter, which were sired by Ch. Bernmont Murdoch. Bred by Andrew Silver.

The litter at five weeks.

A member of the litter at eight weeks.

Silversaints Boffy Bear now aged six months.

bottle-fed puppies to eat meat, before teaching them to lap. They always seem more stupid than naturally fed puppies. Of course, they are not – they are just more used to looking upwards for the bottle, and they do not understand why you are pushing their head downwards in order to lap. If you push the puppy's head gently into the milk, it will get the message in time. To begin with, the puppies make a terrible mess when you put a bowl down for them, and they always seems to put their feet in it. However, their mother will clean them up. We put some Farex or rusk in with the milk as soon as they have learned to lap. When you feel the puppies' teeth starting to come through, which is usually when they are three weeks of age, it is time to introduce some solid food. We feed finely minced meat or tripe, or a good-quality tinned meat puppy food. To start with, get a small piece of food on your finger and encourage the puppy to lick it. It will soon get the idea of chewing the food. Allow each puppy to eat as much as it wants – just make sure their stomachs do not become too full. From this stage they will gradually progress to eating from a dish. If you are feeding a complete dried food you will have to make it very mushy initially, but be guided by the manufacturer's instructions. Always use a good quality complete feed – do not be tempted to go for the cheapest you can find. We have found that complete foods do not produce heavy puppies; the growth-rate tends to be much slower, and the pups do not have much flesh on them. However, they often finish bigger than dogs that are fed on fresh food.

Puppies should be fed five times a day to start with, and then by five weeks of age this should be reduced to four feeds, and a mixer biscuit should be added to the meat. The biscuit should be soaked until it is soft, before it is served. Puppies of this age should never be fed on an exclusive diet of meat. Meat is very low in calcium and Vitamin E, which is important for fertility and muscle function, and the growing pups need a good biscuit mixed in to provide a balanced diet. Sterilised feeding bone-flour can be added, but do not over-do it: too much is as bad as too little and over-supplementation of vitamins and calcium can cause bone deformities. Meat should be fed at the ratio of two-thirds meat or tripe to one-third biscuit meal. High quality tinned puppy foods contain all the necessary vitamins, and you should not need to provide vitamin additives. However, puppies fed on tinned foods do not put on the weight of those fed on fresh meat, though this does not necessarily bear any relation to the size they grow to. We like to start our puppies off on top quality tinned meat, and then switch to a complete food, just adding a small amount of meat to flavour. Some puppies thrive on any sort of food, others can go wrong no matter what you give them; this is the problem with rearing a very large breed such as the St Bernard.

If you are feeding milk, biscuit and meat the puppies should be kept on four feeds a day until they are about three months of age. At eight weeks of age they should be eating approximately one pound of meat and half a pound of biscuit, with bone meal, divided between two meals. The other two meals should consist of milk-feeds, with eggs or cereal added. Fresh water should be available at all times, whichever type of diet you are feeding, but dogs fed on complete diets tend to drink much more water. Food rations should be increased according to demand. However, you must make sure that a puppy does not get too fat and heavy; if a growing dog is carrying excess weight it can be bad for the legs.

By three months of age, most puppies will have left the litter and will be settling in their new homes. At this stage a puppy should be fed a meat meal, morning and evening, with one milk feed in the middle of the day. All breeders have their own methods of feeding, and when you buy a puppy you should continue feeding the diet recommended by the breeder for the first few days, at least. Rely on your own common sense and introduce a change if the puppy is failing to thrive. For example, too much milk can sometimes give a puppy diarrhoea. Some breeders believe that a puppy does not need any milk after it is weaned, but it is a good source of calcium, as well as food. The growing youngster should be kept on three meals a day until it is at least six months old, but preferably continue with this routine until it is nine months old when the majority of dogs will have attained their full height. Use your own judgement: if your puppy looks hungry – providing that it is not overweight – give it more food. If you are feeding a complete diet it is better to give the dog two meals a day, even when it is fully grown. If you are feeding the diet dry, it is essential to have fresh water available at all times. Water should always be available, no matter what you are feeding, but if a dog eats dry food without access to water the dog will draw fluid from its body to compensate and could become seriously dehydrated. Dogs that are fed a dry diet often lack body weight, and so it can be advantageous to soak the food. The traditional method of feeding, i.e. meat or tripe and biscuits, is still preferred by many breeders, but if you are feeding this diet you will need to add vitamins to the food, especially for an in-whelp bitch or an elderly dog. An average diet would consist of 3-4lb of meat or tripe with 1-1½lb of biscuit meal.

Puppies should be allowed ample free exercise. They should play and rest as they wish, but they should not be given forced exercise for long periods – just sufficient to allow for lead training and socialising. An eight-week-old puppy should appear square and sound. If it is going to suffer rear leg problems, these usually start at about three and a half months. However, St Bernards can appear very leggy and loose-jointed while they are growing and then finish up perfectly sound.

With a big breed such as the St Bernard, you may find it useful to provide a kennel. This does not mean the dog has to be in it day and night – but there are always times when it will have to be left, and no matter how much you love your dog, there are times when a giant-sized Saint can get underfoot! The ideal kennel for a St Bernard would be brick or stone-built, approximately eight foot by six foot, and about six foot high – it is not easy to clean out a low kennel. The kennel should have a steel door, and there should be an enclosed exercise area. We have found that weldmesh is the best material for enclosing the run; it lasts longer than chain-link fencing – and an ingenious, persistent dog can escape if only one link is damaged. A bored St Bernard can turn a wooden door into matchwood in a very short space of time, so the ideal kennel should be like Colditz: elephant-proof and mole-proof. If the kennel has a concrete floor – which is the easiest for cleaning – the dog should be provided with a raised board or bed to lie on. The exercise area should be slabbed or concreted. If you use concrete it will need to be sealed, as fresh concrete causes foot abscesses, possibly due to the dust. A grass run looks very nice, but in bad weather it soon turns to mud, and a dog could dig its way out. If you are away for long periods, always leave fresh water readily available for the dog to drink. We would add that not all St Bernards are Houdinis; we are just pointing out the worst you could encounter. A Saint is extremely strong and is therefore capable of wrecking a kennel that is made out of perishable material, if they have a mind to. However, if a puppy is put into a kennel for short periods, it will get used to it and be perfectly content. Make sure that when a dog is left out in its run, it has protection from the sun at all times of the day.

Chapter Thirteen

ST BERNARD COLLECTABLES

Collecting St Bernard memorabilia is often a pastime of St Bernard fanciers worldwide. Ornaments are produced in all manner of materials, from plaster of Paris, earthenware and china, to bronze and silver. There are paintings, postcards and prints showing the St Bernard in a variety of different situations. Visitors to our house are fascinated by our collection of St Bernard ornaments, which must number over a hundred, and is one of the largest in Britain. We also have a collection of St Bernard crested beakers. Pat used to do some sculpting, and she has made several St Bernard models which we have reproduced and marketed in brass or bronze – our brass St Bernard door-knocker is a favourite. We have several paintings, including a print of Sir Edwin Landseer's 'The Rescue'. Landseer was one of the best known animal painters in the 19th Century, and he painted several St Bernards. It was Landseer's 'The Rescue', showing a St Bernard with a brandy barrel round its neck, that contributed to the breed's popularity, and today most St Bernard owners like to have their dogs photographed wearing a brandy barrel. Michael has a special collection of brandy barrels, though it has to be said, most St Bernards do not like wearing them! Arthur Elsley (1860-1952) featured the St Bernard on many of his paintings, and these have been reproduced on greeting cards.

Of course, the shops at the Hospice, and in towns en route in Switzerland and Italy, have many St Bernard souvenirs. Unfortunately, many of these are of poor quality

'The Rescue' Sir Edwin Landseer

'The Rescue Party' Arthur J Elsley   *The Medici Society, London.*

and are mass produced for the fast-growing tourist market. There are many small wooden carvings of St Bernards in Switzerland, but they are usually very expensive, and they are not as detailed as some of the old carvings that can occasionally be found. Genuine barrels are not so easy to come by, as there are very few coopers – the craftsmen who make barrels – still working, and the majority of firms are not tooled up for anything small enough for the dog's neck – although most St Bernard clubs know where to locate them.

Collectables are a good source of income for breed clubs, and nearly all St Bernard clubs have their own metal badges, car stickers and badges, and cloth or blazer badges. There is also a growing market in ties, headscarves, T-shirts, jumpers, aprons and tea-towels printed with a St Bernard design. There is a firm in America that does a special St Bernard watch, and Saints have been featured in jewellery for brooches, pendants, charms and even ear-rings. The English St Bernard Club often gives china with its emblem for trophies at its club shows, and it also sells St Bernard crested china, including a recent limited edition issue of one hundred hand-painted plates. The English St Bernard Club also has several silver St Bernard trophies, which are the envy of many a collector. They were given to the first English breed club – the National St Bernard Club – a hundred years ago. They are collectively valued at £50,000, but it is doubtful whether there is a craftsman that could make them today. These trophies are awarded annually, and kept by the winner for twelve months.

Royal Doulton have produced St Bernards figures in the past, and the older ones are now very valuable. Today the Beswick model comes from the Royal Doulton factory. Other British manufacturers of Saint ornaments include Sylvac, Jaffa Rose, Border Fine Arts, North Light, Melba and Coopercraft and Wade. Italy has produced a number of life-sized figures. The Goebels factory in Germany, and Bisque in France are also well known for their model St Bernards. There are many good plaster models produced in America, as well as more expensive items. Some St Bernard owners confine their collections to antiques, while others have a mixed collection. In England a mixed collection was recently valued at £14,000.

There were magnificent collections on show at the Swiss Centenary Show in 1984, and at the German Centenary Show in 1991. The Swiss covered the entire spectrum of St Bernard collectables, while the German show concentrated on the older and more valuable items. 'Barry', the most famous working St Bernard, is now stuffed and has pride of place in the National History Museum in Berne, Switzerland, and he was lent to the Swiss St Bernard Club for their Centenary Show. Barry has been featured on many postcards – we have a print of him with his head hanging down. When the model became very tatty he was remodelled and stuffed to look as he does

Amanda Gwilliam with Ch. Coatham Star Shine, who has a Hennessy Cognac barrel round its neck.

China plate 1850. Hospice of the Great Saint Bernard.

Left: The 100 Guineas Trophy.

Right: The Abbotspass Trophy .Property of the English St Bernard Club.

today, with his head held high in a proud posture. It is interesting to note that he was not as large or heavy in bone as the present-day St Bernard.

We bought a very nice St Bernard in china in Switzerland, and curiously, it is dated 1942. It stands on a ceramic base and the writing underneath is in Dutch. We have often wondered why someone was making St Bernard ornaments in wartime. We also saw a variety of soft-toy Saints, which are obviously a great favourite with children. They come in all sizes: we saw one on the way to the Hospice which was about double the size of an adult St Bernard. It cost more than a live puppy – although it would not need feeding!

Chapter Fourteen

GENERAL AILMENTS

There are many canine diseases which all breeds may suffer from, and in many cases no one knows how, or why they are contracted. The viral diseases such as distemper/hardpad, leptospirosis, hepatitis, parvovirus and rabies should never occur, as there is effective vaccination available, excluding rabies, in the United Kingdom. As the UK is rabies-free, vaccination is only available for animals going for export. All dogs should be vaccinated as soon as possible. Vets vary as to when they will start a course of vaccination, but it is usually when a puppy is between eight to twelve weeks of age. There is a reluctance to start the course earlier, as puppies should have a natural immunity from their mother in the first few weeks of life. The immunity is passed to the puppies in the colostrum – the mother's milk – in the first twenty-four hours after birth. Orphan puppies may lack this immunity. Vaccinations should be boosted every twelve months throughout a dog's life, and this should never be neglected.

Kennel cough is a viral disease, and there is a vaccination available. However, it has limited protection, as there are many strains of kennel cough in the same way as there are many types of human 'flu. Dogs can get cancer in any of their organs, just as humans can. Some years ago bone cancer seemed very prevalent in St Bernards in the UK, but it does not seem quite as common of late, and there is some treatment available at the veterinary colleges. As the St Bernard is such a large, heavy breed, they are more prone to some bone conditions than most breeds.

HIP DYSPLASIA

This is considered to be only partly hereditary, with environment and feeding playing a large part in its development. It is a condition where the hip joint, which is a ball and socket joint, does not fit properly into the pelvis. In cases of HD, either the ball of the femur, or the socket of the pelvic joint – or both – are misshapen. This occurs, to a certain degree, in the majority of St Bernards, and can cause varying degrees of lameness. Generally, only severe cases cause problems, and these can be assisted by surgery. The muscles in the back legs can be cut, or the hip joint can be replaced in extreme cases, although this is not really to be recommended in a dog as heavy as a St Bernard. Dogs that suffer from severe hip dysplasia should not be used for breeding.

TORN CRUCIATE LIGAMENT

This is another condition that affects the hindlegs. It occurs when the ligament either breaks or stretches. This can be repaired by surgery, either using the dog's own flesh, or using carbon fibre. The condition can often be detected when a previously sound dog goes lame and hangs its hindleg, with the toes just touching the floor. The problem needs rectifying quickly, because the longer you leave it, the more chance there is of arthritis developing in the joint. Some vets will repair it themselves, others will refer it to a veterinary college as it is quite a specialised operation. After-care is all-important. The dog must have controlled walking on a lead while it is recuperating, even when it goes out into the garden to be clean. If the dog runs off, or has any lively exercise before the ligament is healed, it can easily break again. This is not a hereditary condition, and strangely, it is often the sounder dogs that break the cruciate ligaments, possibly because they are more active and agile.

ARTHRITIS

This is an inflammation of the joints, generally occurring in the older dog. The pain can be eased with anti-inflammatory drugs.

SLACK PASTERNS

This is a condition which usually affects puppies from about eight to sixteen weeks. The tendency to suffer from it appears to be partly hereditary, but it is lack of exercise and vitamin deficiency that are influential, and it can be aggravated by a puppy carrying excess weight. Treatment consists of calcium supplementation. This must be under veterinary supervision: too much supplementation can cause as much damage as too little. The puppy also requires exercise – free not forced. If the dog does not come up on its pasterns while it is still young, the condition is unlikely to improve as an adult. Supplementing with Vitamin C is helpful in many disorders, as it helps to assimilate other vitamins.

OSTEOCHONDROSIS DISSECANS

It is only in recent years that this condition has become apparent, and it usually affects the larger, fast-growing breeds. It is not really known why it occurs; it sometimes appears to be more prevalent where there has been an over-supplementation of vitamins, but nothing has been proved. It can affect several joints, but most frequently occurs in the shoulder and the elbow. A piece of bone breaks off and causes the problem. It can settle as the dog gets older, but surgery is usually necessary as if the condition is left untreated, arthritis can develop, particularly in the elbow. Occasional lameness is often a symtom as the piece of bone moves about, and it causes varying degrees of discomfort.

INTERDIGITAL CYSTS

These are small cysts that occur between the toes; sometimes they are caused by a grass-seed or some other foreign body. They can become infected and cause a bad abscess. Bathing and antibiotic treatment usually remedies the condition, although cysts can sometimes recur.

EYE CONDITIONS

ENTROPION

This is more common among the heavy-headed type of St Bernard in Britain, and it also occurs on dogs with a small eye. The eyelashes turn in and rub on the cornea, causing ulceration. If it is not corrected by surgery the cornea will rupture, and the dog may lose its sight. The condition can be present in one or both eyes, on the top or the bottom lid, or both. The operation to correct it involves the vet taking a piece of flesh of the correct shape, above or below the eye, depending on which lids are affected. If the vet is not very experienced in this particular operation, it would be wise to ask to be referred to a veterinary college. If the wrong shape or size of flesh is removed, it can ruin the dog's appearance. Care must also be taken after the operation to prevent the dog from scratching its stitches. An Elizabethan collar can be used, but this sometimes aggravates the dog more, and a light sedative for the first few days following the operation is often easier and more effective.

ECTROPION

This is also a common problem among British St Bernards, and it seems to affect those with droopy eyes. In this case the eyelids turn outwards, but this does not cause as much damage as entropion. However, if the eye is too open, it can be exposed to infection.

ENLARGED HARDERIAN GLAND

The gland behind the third eyelid, i.e. the haw, becomes enlarged and ruptures, and appears as a red lump in the corner of the eye. A simple operation will correct it: the lump just needs to be surgically removed.

PROGRESSIVE RETINAL ATROPHY (PRA)

This is the progressive destruction of the light-sensitive tissues at the back of the eye. Symptoms are failing sight in dim light, and eventually total blindness. It is an inherited defect, but it is not a known disease in the St Bernard.

INFECTIOUS DISEASES

DISTEMPER/HARDPAD

Symptoms: diarrhoea, sickness, runny eyes, crystallised nose, then twitching followed by fits.

LEPTOSPIROSIS

This is caused by the bacteria Leptospira icterohaemorrhagiae and leptospira canicola – both can be caught by humans. Leptospira I. is carried by rats. The symptoms are high temperature, thirst, abdominal pain, jaundice, diarrhoea containing blood, and vomiting. Leptospira C. is passed by dogs sniffing urine of infected dogs. It has similar symptoms to Leptospira I., but jaundice is not as marked.

CANINE PARVOVIRUS.

Symptoms: severe sickness and diarrhoea, often with blood content. If the dog is not treated quickly it can dehydrate, and an intravenous drip may be necessary to bring the dog's body fluids back up to normal.

HEPATITIS

This is inflammation of the liver caused by canine adenovirus. It is highly contagious in dogs, but has no connection with hepatitis in humans.
Symptoms: very high temperature, sickness, diarrhoea, possibly yellowing of the eyes.

Veterinary treatment is essential in all of the infectious diseases listed above, but they are extremely difficult to cure. However, they can all be prevented by vaccine.

KENNEL COUGH

Symptoms: husky cough and runny nose. It is highly contagious – the virus can be airborne. A healthy adult dog usually gets over it fairly quickly, although it can cause fatalities in young puppies and old dogs. It can also be extremely harmful to the puppies of a pregnant bitch. Veterinary treatment is essential for the young and old.

HEART DISEASE

Unfortunately, this is quite common in St Bernards. Symptoms can be exhaustion on exercise, or even sudden collapse. If a dog suffers a heart attack, it may also appear to throw its legs about. Veterinary treatment is necessary; many heart conditions can be controlled by medication, which is usually necessary for the rest of the dog's life.

HEAT STROKE

This can occur in hot weather if the dog lies in the sun for too long, or if it is left too long in a hot vehicle. The temperature in a car or van can become unbearable in hot weather in a very short time. When a dog is over-heated, its breathing becomes laboured and is often noisy and rasping. In advanced cases, the tongue can go blue. The dog's temperature needs to be brought down immediately. This can be done by applying ice packs, hosing the dog down with cold water, or putting towels, soaked with cold water, on the head and shoulders. Call the vet as well, but do not wait until he arrives before cooling the dog down, or you could be too late. Never leave any dog outside in the sun without shade. St Bernards tend to feel the heat more than most breeds, and the long-haired suffer more than the short-haired variety.

BLOAT/STOMACH TORSION

This is severe distension of the stomach, caused by the formation of too many gases. It is often caused by stomach torsion; this is a complete twist of the stomach, which prevents the gases from escaping. The dog will try to be sick, but will only bring up froth. This is an emergency, and immediate veterinary treatment is essential. The dog will need an operation to put the stomach back in its rightful position. The swifter the treatment, the better the chance of survival. It is not a condition that can be left – even if it is the middle of the night. All decent vets understand this. Unfortunately, any dog that does survive the operation is a prime candidate for the condition to recur. The dog will need feeding little and often, for the rest of its life. Some vets stitch the stomach to the abdominal wall to prevent the condition recurring, but many do not like to do this. Torsion cannot be classed as a hereditary condition as such, but some lines do seem to be more prone to it than others.

DIARRHOEA

This is a symptom of many diseases, but it can also occur on its own, caused by infection or a change of food. Diarrhoea in young puppies, particularly accompanied by sickness, should never be treated lightly, as they can soon dehydrate. Kaolin and morphine suspension can help to stop the diarrhoea, but if the trouble persists, veterinary treatment should be sought.

CONSTIPATION

This can be caused by eating too many bones, or too much bone-flour, particularly in young puppies. Liquid paraffin is a useful laxative, but if this does not work, there could be an obstruction.

SICKNESS

Dogs often eat grass and bring it back, just to clean their stomachs, and this is no cause for alarm. Occasionally they are sick if they eat too quickly, but any persistent sickness should not be left unattended. An excessive thirst accompanied by vomiting is often a forerunner of bloat.

CYSTITIS

This is inflammation of the bladder often caused by a chill, particularly in young puppies. The dog will continually try to pass water, or it may keep passing water in small quantities. The condition can be swiftly treated by a vet.

METRITIS

This is an inflammation or infection of the womb following pregnancy. Symptoms are a brown or blackish discharge, and general malaise. It can be caused by the bitch failing to give birth to a dead puppy. Providing there is neither puppy nor placenta retained in the uterus, it can be cleared up with antibiotic treatment from your vet.

PYOMETRA

This is an infection of the womb which generally starts about three weeks after the bitch's season. It often starts with a thick, pink smelly discharge. Sometimes antibiotics can help, but usually removal of the womb (hysterectomy) is necessary in order for the bitch to make a full recovery.

ECLAMPSIA

Commonly known as milk fever, this can occur two to three days after whelping. It is caused by a calcium deficiency in the blood stream. The bitch appears very restless at the onset, and then she may fall about, and finally collapse. The veterinary surgeon can inject a calcium solution into the vein, which will bring about an immediate recovery, but further treatment will possibly be necessary to prevent reoccurrence.

MASTITIS

This is an inflammation of the mammary glands, and it is often caused by too much milk in the nursing mother. It is characterised by a hard lump in the bitch's breasts. It should be treated with antibiotics.

PARASITES

INTERNAL

ROUNDWORMS: All dogs should be wormed regularly to keep them in good condition. Puppies need worming against roundworms from the age of two weeks onwards (with a paste from the vet), then every two weeks until the puppy is three months of age, and then again at six months, and two weeks later to clear any undeveloped eggs. From then onwards, a dog should be wormed twice yearly.

TAPEWORMS: This is the other type of worm common in the United Kingdom. It is a flat, segmented worm, which affects the small intestines. Small white segments can appear in the faeces. The vet will prescribe tablets, according to the weight of the dog.

HEARTWORMS: This parasite can be a problem to dogs in the U.S.A. The worm is passed from dog to dog through mosquito bites. It can take from eight to nine months from the time of the bite until the heartworm is mature. As eradication is extremely difficult; veterinary consultation is important.

WHIPWORMS AND HOOKWORMS: These are also common in the U.S.A. and a vet's help should be sought to eradicate them.

EXTERNAL

FLEAS, LICE, TICKS AND MITES: These can be eradicated either by dusting with a louse powder at frequent intervals, or by regular spraying with an insecticidal spray. Regular bathing with an insecticidal bath is equally effective, but always remember to treat the dog's bedding as well. Flea collars can also be used; it is often necessary to fasten two together to fit a St Bernard, and cut off any excess. However, dogs can sometimes be allergic to these collars, so it is wise to check regularly to see if the skin is becoming irritated. If this is the case, the flea collar should be removed immediately. Ticks are often picked up from fields where sheep have been grazing. If you touch a tick with paraffin, it will withdraw its head, and so the entire tick can then be removed.

SARCOPTIC MANGE

This is s a parasitic disease whereby mites burrow under the skin. Regular powdering with a louse powder can eradicate these, but controlled regular bathing in a special shampoo, or medication available from your vet, is more effective, particularly on the short-haired Saints. It is also cleaner to use, especially if the dog lives in the house.

DERMODACTIC MANGE

This is caused by a microscopic mite which is a normal inhabitant of canine hair follicles, and usually it does not cause problems. However, sometimes the mites multiply causing hair-loss and dermatitis. It is more common in short-haired dogs. Sometimes secondary bacterial infection can occur. Veterinary treatment should be sought.

EAR CANKER

The ears can also be invaded by a small mite, and any infection can cause ear canker. There are various medications available, but the ears should be cleaned out regularly as part of a general management programme.

POISONS

There are many poisons which a dog can take by accident, or even lick off its feet. Anti-freeze, paint-remover, lead paints, glue and creosote, detergents, and disinfectants are all toxic. All rat and mouse poisons, weedkillers and slug pellets are very poisonous.

There are also many plants or parts of plants that are poisonous to the dog. These include: Deadly Nightshade, with its purple flowers and black berries, the seeds from a Laburnum tree, Hyacinth, Narcissi, Daffodil, and autumn Crocus bulbs; underground stems of Iris and Lily of the Valley; Mistletoe berries, Foxglove leaves (source of the Digitalis drug used for heart conditions); Rhubarb, Oleander, and Poinsetta leaves; all parts of Laurels,; Rhododendrons and Azaleas; Yew; and the twigs of the wild and cultivated Cherry trees.

Care should always be taken when you are walking in the countryside to make sure your dog does not drink from any puddles, as these could be contaminated from chemicals or sprays. Dogs could also be affected by chemical spray, if they should run through a field of crops. If a dog has been out in the fields at spraying time, wash their feet well in warm water and dry them, before they have a chance to lick them. If you think your dog has eaten or drunk a poisonous substance, try to make it vomit, and then get it to the vet as soon as possible.